the
PRINCESS
BITCHFACE
SYNDROME 2.0

Michael Carr-Greg is an adolescent psychologist, a well-respected speaker and one of Australia's leading authorities on teenage behaviour. In 1985 he founded CanTeen, the acclaimed cancer patients' support group for teenagers in New Zealand and Australia. He is the consultant psychologist to many schools and national organisations, and has written several books on parenting adolescents.

Elly Robinson is a researcher, writer and mother who began her career as a youth worker. Since then she has worked to promote the use of evidence in practice with children, young people and families. She has a Graduate Diploma in Adolescent Health and a Master of Public Health from the University of Melbourne.

the
PRINCESS
BITCHFACE
SYNDROME 2.0

DR MICHAEL CARR-GREGG
AND ELLY ROBINSON

PENGUIN BOOKS

PENGUIN BOOKS

UK | USA | Canada | Ireland | Australia
India | New Zealand | South Africa | China

Penguin Books is part of the Penguin Random House group of companies
whose addresses can be found at global.penguinrandomhouse.com.

Penguin
Random House
Australia

First published by Penguin Random House Australia Pty Ltd, 2006
This edition published by Penguin Australia Pty Ltd, 2017

Text copyright © Michael Carr-Gregg and Elly Robinson 2017

The moral right of the author has been asserted.

Cover design by Alex Ross © Penguin Random House Australia Pty Ltd
Text design by Louisa Maggio © Penguin Random House Australia Pty Ltd
Cover photograph by PhotoAlto/Laurence Mouton/Getty Images
Typeset in Adobe Casion by Louisa Maggio, Penguin Random House Australia Pty Ltd
Printed and bound in Australia by Griffin Press, an accredited ISO AS/NZS 14001
Environmental Management Systems printer.

National Library of Australia
Cataloguing-in-Publication data:

Carr-Gregg, Michael, author.
The princess bitchface syndrome 2.0 / Michael Carr-Gregg;
Elly Robinson.
9780143784265 (paperback)
Subjects: Teenage girls.
Parent and teenager.
Adolescent psychology.

Other Creators/Contributors:
Robinson, Elly, 1968– author.

penguin.com.au

Contents

Preface

So why write a new edition of *The Princess Bitchface Syndrome*? Well for a start, the phenomenon is still alive and well, but there is a twist in the tale – and it is digital. Back in 2006, the internet and social media were almost nonexistent. In 2017, any meaningful discussion of the parenting of teenage girls cannot avoid acknowledging the impact of their online world and how parents can manage it – hence PBS2.0!

Since I wrote PBS in 2006 I have continued my clinical practice, but have also worked as Managing Director of the Young and Well Cooperative Research Centre, set up by the Federal Government to examine how new and emerging technologies might impact on young people. In writing this new edition, I have enlisted an old friend, Elly Robinson, who is a wonderful writer and researcher, but is also someone I have worked with for a very long time. Together we have written an updated, enhanced and much better version of the first book, but for clarity we've kept it in my voice. So pour yourself a chardonnay, put your feet up, turn your phone to silent and read on ...

Dr Michael Carr-Gregg
Melbourne
January 2017

Introduction

Many people who picked up this book for the first time in 2006 found the title objectionable, so I felt the need to explain where it came from. A 30-something friend of mine, Nikki, was enjoying a fairly 'robust' relationship with her teenage daughter. Nikki explained to me that she was particularly envious of a friend who insisted on waxing lyrical about how quiet, helpful and studious her own adolescent daughter was. Then one day Nikki attended a school morning tea and, anticipating the latest rant with a slightly heavy heart, ambled over to the mother of this paragon of virtue. She asked politely how the other woman's daughter was. Nikki was more than a little surprised by her response: 'You mean Princess Bitchface?'

Clearly the puberty fairy had arrived and left a very special type of teenager under this parent's pillow . . .

I admitted back then – and still hold the view – that there are plenty of teenage girls who rise early and get ready for their day without behaving like total brats.

But if you listen to parents and teachers, as I do on a regular basis, you would have to agree that there are some girls whose behaviour seems, for a period of time, to be like a direct emotional assault. Virtually overnight, they transform into a rebellious stranger, spitting venom and slamming doors if you remind them to do their homework, make their own lunch or bring out their dirty washing. Alongside this, I often see mother–daughter relationships with a veneer of contentment that is nothing more than illusion. The reality is a household divided by torrid encounters, where parents are forever sucked into an emotional vortex characterised by a chaos that in many cases the parents exacerbate in their attempts to *avert* chaos.

I decided, back in 2006, to call this manifestation of development in teenage girls the Princess Bitchface Syndrome. In psychology, the word 'syndrome' refers to a collection of signs and/or symptoms that together form a condition with a known outcome, or that requires a special response. And the key here is that parents do need to act. We might think that the cumulative experiences of a child prior to adolescence are far more important, but we can't drop the ball in the teenage years. Now is the time to reinforce all the good lessons learned in childhood, and to prepare your teenager to be increasingly responsible for her own health and wellbeing – while understanding why she won't always listen to what you have to say.

When you look at the list of developmental tasks of adolescence, it's no wonder this is such a time of turmoil. The teenager is beginning to:

- achieve emotional independence from parents and other adults
- develop a realistic, stable, positive identity
- form a gender identity
- cultivate positive and healthy peer and intimate relationships
- develop a realistic body image
- formulate a moral/value system
- acquire skills for future economic independence.

Many factors will influence the timing of and extent to which these developmental tasks are achieved. Parents obviously play an important role, but so do factors such as the teen's temperament and personality, the quality of her friendships, the nature of the school environment, and the influence of extended family. And you don't need to be the Agony Uncle for a teenage girls' magazine to realise that life for young women is tougher than ever before. Many eminent psychologists, such as Lisa Damour, maintain that girls today feel pressure to be 'successful in school, friendly, helpful, physically attractive, athletic, and popular'. That's a lot to ask of any human being, let alone a young person entwined in intricate peer relationships who is also dealing with questions of identity, sexuality and self-worth. And whether we are aware of it or not, those of us who surround teenage girls often inadvertently communicate such expectations.

These expectations also occur against a backdrop of shifting demographic trends, which add even more pressure to these young women. Today's teenage girls are now more likely than the previous generation to live in a smaller household with fewer siblings and with both parents working. As a result, many girls not only have less access to positive role models in older siblings, but also have time-poor parents who take the path of least resistance, avoiding discipline and overindulging their daughters. In addition, around 40 per cent of marriages end in divorce and almost half of these involve children, meaning that many young women are either living in single-parent households – most often with their mothers and seeing less of their fathers – or in blended families with all the complexities of dealing with step-parents and step-siblings.

The pressure on young women is reflected in health and wellbeing statistics. The most recent national survey of child and adolescent mental health and wellbeing, conducted by the University of Western Australia, showed that around 1 in 8 young women aged 12–17 has been diagnosed with a mental disorder, with 1 in 5 aged 16–17 meeting diagnostic criteria for major depressive disorder. Studies indicate that intentional self-harm is also on the rise, with young women aged 15–24 representing one-third of all females hospitalised for intentional self-harm in 2012–13. Three-quarters of secondary school girls wished they were thinner, and half have tried to lose weight. One in 10 young women aged 12–17 and almost 1 in 4 aged 18–24 has used illicit drugs.

While I don't doubt the love that parents have for their daughters, I am not convinced that many understand them well enough to offer the kind of support and guidance these young women need on their journey to independence. Indeed, some parents can be so overwhelmed by their daughter's behaviour that they take the path of least resistance and simply give in to her every whim. As we will see, this has dire consequences for her social and emotional development, not least of which is her ability to cope when life doesn't turn out the way she planned.

Clearly, the days of blind obedience, deep and abiding respect and automatic compliance from our offspring are far off in the dusty past (were they ever here?). It is quite simply not possible to 'control' our children (or anyone for that matter!). Such an approach will only invite conflict and increased resistance. But giving up is not an option, either.

You may think you have been consigned to a meta-phorical garbage bin of irrelevance and irritation, but she needs you to believe in her and to trust that she will get through this, and yet be strong enough to set limits that keep her safe. Young people need rules and boundaries if they are to internalise a moral code. So while it is vital that you are supportive and loving, you still need to know where she is, who she is with and what she is doing.

I have written this book to help you better understand your adolescent daughter so that you can parent with intelligence and with a loving but firm hand. In Part 1, I explain how the experience of puberty (with its whirlwind of physical, mental, emotional and social changes) influences your daughter's moods and behaviour, and also how other factors in her world (at home, at school and online) can shape whether outcomes are positive or negative.

In Part 2, I discuss tried and true strategies to help parents cope with the demands of raising recalcitrant teens, including setting boundaries, implementing pre-agreed consequences, using reflective listening and managing your own anger. I also look at everyday issues for parents of any teenager, such as sleep, technology, curfews and sibling rivalry, as well as more challenging issues such as bullying, drug and alcohol abuse, self-harm and depression. To be clear, these more challenging issues may arise with *any* teenager, not just Princess B, and will depend on the particular balance of risk and protective factors in a young person's life. Risk factors include having a relative with mental illness, conflict at home, low achievement at school and being disconnected from peers. Protective factors include being good at something (finding her 'spark') and having an adult mentor.

So before we move on, let's just remind ourselves that there is no such thing as a perfect parent. We can only do what we do, with what we know at the time. So whether you are just about to hop on the rollercoaster of teenage girldom, or are already flying through the air with your arms akimbo, this book will help you parent with greater confidence and understanding.

Part 1

What's up with Princess B?

Chapter 1

Meet Matilda

It is a Saturday afternoon, and 13-year-old Matilda
has been out in the city with friends. Her mother,
Sylvie, is starting to worry as Matilda was due home
at 4 p.m. and is now 45 minutes late and is not
answering her texts. She is just considering calling
the mother of one of Matilda's friends when she hears
the front door slam and the clamorous thumping of
Doc Marten boots up the hallway. Sylvie grits her
teeth, dreading the thought of another confrontation
with her increasingly moody daughter.

Suddenly she hears the sound of raucous squealing
and peals of laughter – Matilda has brought her
friends Rhianna and Sadie home. Sylvie can feel her
shoulders starting to tense up. Matilda knows that
Sylvie wouldn't have wanted her to bring friends home
unannounced at this time of day. Just another in the
long list of things she seems to do purposely these days
to defy Sylvie's authority (and seriously piss her off!).

The trio flounce into the living room, where Sylvie

is working on her computer and Sammy, Matilda's younger brother, is contentedly playing Minecraft on the couch. Matilda flicks her brother's ear hard and yells at him to get off her new iPad (bought by her father prior to his latest work trip overseas). Sammy yelps and tries to slap Matilda. As she deftly moves out of harm's way, her friends titter appreciatively and tug at the sleeves of Sylvie's brand new Country Road top that Matilda has helpfully removed from its packaging and worn today.

Matilda turns and tries to sit on Sammy, who, amidst a barrage of invective, leaps up, storms out of the living room and slams his bedroom door. Matilda is yet to acknowledge her mother's presence beyond a vague wave in her direction when her mother says hello. She pats the couch on either side of her and Rhianna and Sadie dutifully sit down. Sadie starts to plait Matilda's hair before Matilda squeals in outrage and slaps Sadie's hand away. Rhianna, who seems a quiet and pleasant girl whenever she is free of Matilda's company, looks up to see Sylvie's response. Matilda picks up the iPad Sammy was happily using moments earlier, squeals again enthusiastically for no apparent reason and downloads the latest videos on her Musical.ly account. She cranks up the iPad to maximum volume and groans loudly at Rhianna's latest attempts to mime a recent hit, before turning to Rhianna and calling her a 'dumb bitch'.

Sylvie jerks her head up. She feels her heart start to pound, but she knows she must respond even though she is entirely familiar with what will come next. 'Mattie', she says carefully, 'it is not okay to speak to your friends that way.'

Matilda slowly turns her head and glares at her mother. 'BUT SHE IS!' Matilda screams. 'She's totally wrecking the song! Even someone as old and wrinkled as you can see that!' Matilda gets up, shoves the iPad directly under her mother's nose and presses play.

Matilda's two friends hover behind her, unsure of what to do and where to look. Rhianna seems close to tears. Sylvie instinctively pushes the iPad away and looks back at her own computer screen. She takes a deep breath as Matilda hovers menacingly above her. 'Matilda, I'm busy finishing this report right now. You need to apologise to Rhianna, say goodbye to your friends and start setting the table for dinner.'

Matilda looks at her mother incredulously, as if she had just asked her to bathe all the residents at the local aged care facility. She looks around to make sure her friends are watching, then yells, 'Dinner smells DISGUSTING! I'm not eating it!' Matilda twists on one heel, flicks her hair and disappears off to her bedroom, pulling Rhianna and Sadie along with her. Sylvie takes another deep breath and slowly rises. With her husband away on business until Wednesday, she has no choice but to deal with her teenage daughter alone.

Sylvie knocks on Matilda's bedroom door several times, but remains unheard above the din of Justin Bieber's new ode to another beautiful girl. She finally twists the doorknob and interrupts Matilda changing into a clean set of clothes for the third time today, leaving Sylvie's new top in a crumpled heap on the floor. Matilda screams again. 'MUM, GET OUT! I HATE this stupid house! I HATE YOU and all your stupid RULES! You never let me have any PRIVACY!' She pulls on her boots, storms past her mother (stepping on her big toe for good measure), yanks open the front door and disappears back into the evening. Rhianna and Sadie meekly pass Sylvie and trail after their friend out the door.

Sylvie feels a mixture of anger, grief and humiliation. Where is the happy, compliant, playful little girl she took to the park and played on the swings with, the one who loved spending time with her mum?

Sylvie runs to the door and calls out, 'Matilda!' She knows she cannot chase her – she cannot leave Sammy alone in the house. Matilda doesn't look back.

Sylvie goes back inside the house and tries calling her daughter's mobile, but unsurprisingly there is no answer. She paces up and down the hall for a while, fighting tears and frantically sending her daughter texts, asking her to please come home.

Eventually she calls Sadie's mother, who lives close by. 'Yes, they're here,' Diana says cheerily. 'She's in tears – she said you were yelling at her. Are you okay? The girls are consoling her now. It's fine – she can stay here for dinner. We love Matilda, she's such a sweet girl.'

Matilda, as you've no doubt surmised, is a shining example of Princess Bitchface 2.0. Furious that her mother attempted to set behavioural boundaries in front of her friends, Matilda is determined to teach her mother a lesson. She does this by using a sustained bout of character assassination augmented by yelling, screaming and a barrage of insults, all of which are aimed at: a) impressing her friends so that she can remain the Queen Bee, b) sending a clear message to her mother that Sylvie is *not* the boss and c) letting her mother know that unless she caves in to her demands, she can expect World War Three.

So what should Sylvie have done in this particular situation? Instead of meekly surrendering to Matilda's bullying and disrespectful behaviour, she should have told Sadie's mother *not* to give her dinner and that she would come and collect her. Once at home, she should have sent Matilda to her room with a calm recitation of all the logical and natural consequences of the following poor choices:

a) Missing the curfew for being home
b) Hitting her brother
c) Being disrespectful to her friend
d) Being disrespectful to her mother
e) Leaving home without permission

Of course Sylvie can only do this if she and her husband have already *set* clear boundaries about what is and what is not acceptable behaviour and spoken to Matilda about the consequences of any breach of these rules. Back when this behaviour first emerged, Sylvie should have shut it down, because we teach people how to treat us.

For Sylvie and other parents struggling with a Princess B, it is about grabbing the reins and never allowing their child to drag them into the jungle. To coin my favourite piece of parenting advice, 'Never wrestle with a pig in the mud because you both get dirty and the pig loves it!'

If Sylvie permits her daughter to act this way, it sends a clear message that it is acceptable. And every time Matilda gets away with it, it is reinforced even more.

So what has been going on in Princess B's brain to trigger these outbursts of egocentric behaviour and poor impulse control in the first place? Let me give you a contemporary crash course in the developmental psychology of teenage girls. I believe that knowledge is power, and armed with these princess paradigms you'll have a much better understanding of what is motivating the Matildas of the world to behave this way.

Chapter 2
Puberty

In 2014 there were almost 4.9 million young people aged 10–25 in Australia. That's around one-fifth of the population moving through puberty, adolescence and young adulthood. Though this developmental period has long been regarded as a challenging time for both teenagers and parents, life in the 21st century has provided some additional pressures. While these pressures are not limited to girls, their generally more advanced communication skills (sharply honed in the primary school playground) tend to make them more articulate than their male counterparts about what's going on in their lives.

Generally, puberty refers to the physical changes that transform a child into a sexually developed being, while adolescence is a catch-all term for all the other changes – emotional, psychological and social – that follow in its wake. Adolescence is best understood as a transitional period between childhood and adulthood, characterised by both physical and psychological changes that do not occur on a strict timeline but at different times according to a genetic roadmap unique to each individual. So what sorts of changes occur over this time, and what influences them?

THE TEENAGE BODY

During puberty, two of the main organs of the body, the brain and pituitary gland, release hormones that are responsible for the development of the reproductive organs in both males and females. As a result, children begin to mature biologically, psychologically, socially and cognitively – a process that can take anywhere from one to six years. Everyone matures at their own pace, but eventually they all catch up to one another (although there are exceptions in Hollywood).

For the vast majority of Australian girls, it is a transition with a fairly standard sequence of physical changes. The release of increased quantities of hormones produces an overall growth spurt, the ovaries become active, breasts and body hair develop and menstruation begins. Unlike the slow developmental progress in childhood, change is now rapid and dramatic.

One difference between girls and boys is the different timing of growth spurts and development of 'secondary' sexual characteristics; that is, visible changes such as pubic and facial hair growth and breast or testes enlargement. Girls commonly undergo the general growth spurt before or around the same time that they begin to develop sexually, whereas boys develop sexually first and grow taller later. For girls, a key challenge of adolescence is to adjust to this new physical self: she looks less like a child and more like a young woman, with the result that she often becomes extremely focused on her body. She needs to build a sense of what it means to be female into her unfolding self-image, develop a set of values about sexual behaviour and learn to manage her sexuality.

While there is great variability in the time of onset, velocity of change and the age of completion, children are generally beginning puberty much earlier than in the past. The Avon Longitudinal Study of 14000 children in the UK found 1 in 6 girls began puberty by eight years of age, compared to 1 in 100 a generation ago, and that 1 in 14 eight-year-old boys had pubic hair compared to 1 in 150 a generation ago.

One of the consequences of this early physical maturation is that children can feel confused and overwhelmed by how different they are to their peers, making them more sensitive to stress. Others can look a lot older than they are, and may find themselves in situations that they are not ready to handle. As puberty occurs earlier, it's no longer in synchronisation with brain development, so adolescent psychologists are often confronted with a fully developed young woman, flaunting her rebellion with multiple piercings, but with the cognitive capacity of a 13-year-old. A souped-up car with all the extras – but the driver has no licence. These young people haven't spent long enough just hanging out with their buddies – learning how to manage conflict, make moral choices and solve problems – before they suddenly find themselves with a boyfriend or girlfriend.

Over the last few years, childhood as we know it seems

to have been steadily eroded. Many girls today seem to be going straight from toys to boys, without a stop at the 'tween' years. They can't drive or vote, but have been raised as consumers, with significant spending power. There is unprecedented pressure on young people to grow up much earlier. We can see this reflected in the lack of products that exhibit a true understanding of the challenges and needs of the 'tween' age group; from books and clothes to hair and skin care. Instead of products that are not too childish but still suit a developing body and mind, the 'girls' section of many (online and offline) stores jumps straight from cute cherry-covered dresses to spaghetti-strap singlet tops, push-up bras and 'waist trainers'. It's a direct and unsubtle leap to the teenage years.

THE TEENAGE BRAIN

At birth, we all have more than 100 billion brain cells, more than the number of stars in the Milky Way, but only about 17 per cent of these cells are interconnected – relaying messages that control heartbeat and breathing, reflexes and other basic functions. The brain continues to form connections over the next two decades, in fits and starts, by adding grey matter (neurons, dendrites and synapses), destroying old neural connections and synapses and building new ones – all the time producing the complex circuits that shape our thinking, feelings and behaviour. Matilda and her adolescent counterparts are navigating an internal cyclone, without a map or compass.

For many years, developmental psychologists assumed that the brain was fully formed when the skull reached adult size – that is, by the age of 13–14. But in recent decades, neuroscientists have identified a second growth spurt involving grey matter just before puberty, followed by another bout of 'pruning' during adolescence itself. Pruning is the process whereby the brain gets rid of unnecessary connections and strengthens others that are necessary and important. Many brain regions are pruned early in life and don't change much in later years. But pruning in regions that control higher level cognitive functioning, such as making complex decisions or logical reasoning, is not completed until the mid-20s. This is why there is much less difference in the way people see, hear and walk compared to the ways in which they reason, plan for the future and control their emotions. The extent of our ability to perform high-level cognitive functions such as the latter is heavily shaped by adolescent experiences.

To make up for the shortfall in higher level cognitive functioning, the adolescent relies heavily on another area of the brain, the amygdala. The amygdala is the primitive and instinctive part of the brain and, as such, its use creates a tendency to react automatically to stimulus, often termed the 'fight or flight' response. In other words, adolescents do not have the same ability as adults to control their impulses and make sound decisions, which in turn means there is no point in judging their actions from an adult perspective. This is both unfair and unhelpful, and will inevitably lead to disappointment.

Princess B is on her way to acquiring incredible new skill sets, especially when it comes to social behaviour and abstract thought. But in the process of testing these skills, she will often use her parents as guinea pigs. Typically, Princess B will see initiating conflict as a type of self-expression, and she may have trouble focusing on an abstract idea or empathising with her target's feelings. This can help to explain her apparent self-centredness and selfish behaviour.

Princess B's brain is hardwired to seek reward, act out, be influenced by peers and otherwise exhibit immaturity, and this *will* change when she becomes an adult. As additional areas of the brain start to help process emotion, older teenagers gain some equilibrium and everyone in the family has an easier time. But in the heat of the teenage moment, decision-making can be overly guided by emotions and peer pressure as opposed to rational decisions, which she is not yet fully capable of.

This is best represented by the duality in the teenage years of behaving in a certain way (e.g. taking drugs, driving too fast, shoplifting) even though they can explain precisely why this is not a good choice. This can be very confusing for parents, but is symptomatic of this stage of development. Teenage brains are wired to seek reward, and they need higher doses of risk to feel the same 'rush' that adults do. This may make them vulnerable to engaging in increasingly risky behaviours.

An example of this is young people's driving behaviours. Research, released by the Australian Institute of Family Studies in 2013, showed that 43 per cent of people aged 19–20 had been involved in a crash, while almost a third had been detected speeding by police at least once. Two-thirds reported driving while very tired. By the time these young people were 24 years old, 1 in 5 admitted to driving near or over the legal limit for alcohol use. These statistics make sense when you consider that *30 per cent* of all deaths in young people are as a result of transport accidents, compared to *1 per cent* of people aged 25 years or over.

The whole point of this section is that adult carers need to understand that no matter how tall their daughter is, or how grown-up she appears, she is still in a developmental period that will affect the rest of her life. Princess B's experiences – from reading teen vampire novels to learning to drive – continually shape new grey matter. Adolescence, therefore, is a critical time of 'use it and improve it'. Development at this stage of life is stimulated most effectively when there is a slight mismatch between what we can do already and when we push ourselves to do a little better. If your daughter does a lot of reading, she will become a better reader; if she regularly plays the piano when young, she will become a better pianist. What she uses and learns in school will become hardwired into the brain's structure – but what she ignores will lose its priority. This is why exposing adolescents to as many positive and novel challenges at this age is so important for building the skills they will need in the adult world.

With all this restructuring going on, is it any wonder that the teenage brain is at times disorganised, impulsive and prone to misunderstanding by others? Understanding brain development is a key component of parenting teenagers generally, but especially those with an XY chromosome. Girls are more emotional, manipulative and moody than their male counterparts. Unfortunately for parents of more demanding daughters, female brains are predisposed to excel in language, listening skills, fine motor skills and attention to detail. Girls' brains are more 'decentralised', using a variety of different areas for a single task, whereas boys only use one side of their brain and process one thing at a time. Thus for adolescent girls the mix of biological changes, inbuilt brain programming and external factors sets the stage for a confused and sometimes stormy inner world.

> Our 14-year-old daughter seems rational and reason-
> able one minute, but the next she's quite a pain. She
> just doesn't seem to listen to us anymore. She forgets
> things we've asked her to do and accuses us of nagging
> when we remind her. One day we have a decent
> conversation with her and we think, 'Great! That stage
> has passed . . .' But then two days later, she'll be acting
> like a child again.

Your daughter is not necessarily being deliberately obnoxious. As a parent it is helpful to see this as part of the natural development going on in her brain, of which inconsistency is one symptom. Her brain is trying to sort through lots of options and identities – whether she's going to be an academic, an athlete or an artist. As parents, our job is to make sure that the choices she makes don't have irreversible consequences. We need to develop a tolerance of the relatively minor things, and not forget that it is also frustrating for girls themselves – they don't always *choose* to be defiant or disobedient or disorganised.

Chapter 3

The stages of adolescence

So far we've looked at the physiological changes that occur during adolescence. In this chapter, we'll examine the emotional, psychological and social changes that follow in their wake.

Princess B is maturing physically and experiencing new and strange impulses that she doesn't yet know how to handle. Although she is biologically mature, she is not yet an adult in psychological and social terms. So if she behaves like a grown-up one day and a stubborn child the next, it is because she *is* half-child and half-adult. If she loves something one moment and hates it the next, it's because she isn't yet sure *what* she wants. If she is rebellious or challenges your values and rules, it is because she is searching for her own coherent, stable sense of self.

Parents need to think of this journey as an economist would. At first you invest your love and energy, and the returns are great. Middle adolescence can sometimes feel like a recession, as you get little or nothing back. But the good news is that towards the end of the journey (mid-20s) most parents discover not only that their original investment is still there, but also that its value has increased immeasurably.

EARLY ADOLESCENCE

Early adolescence roughly corresponds to ages 10–14 years. A girl at this age can feel gawky and may look awkward as well. This is because her bones, muscles and organs (like those of all adolescents) are growing at different rates, resulting in the classic gangly look of this age group. She is progressing through puberty and is very conscious of the physical changes she's undergoing, which increases her anxiety about her body shape, her growth and her sexuality. She's becoming very sensitive to teasing about her appearance and needs buckets of reassurance that she's normal.

The close friendships formed in early adolescence are best understood as intense mini love affairs, usually based on geographical proximity (though mobiles and internet chatting have made this less important), shared interests and hobbies, or other connections. Girls tend to have fewer, but emotionally closer friends than boys do (for more on cliques, see page 42). At this age, some seem to do nothing more than talk about their latest crush, whereas others just want to watch *Dr Who* marathons. Some have had their first periods, often months ago, while others will not experience periods for months to come. This physical, social, cognitive and emotional variability, alongside the looming transition to high school, leads to the tricky relationships with friends and others so often seen in the final years of primary school.

The early adolescent wavers between wanting to turn away from her childhood and the authority of her parents, and still depending on them – one minute wanting a hug and the next repulsed by any contact. She can be happy in the morning but deeply upset by the afternoon, even though nothing seems to have happened. There is no shortage of low-voltage conflict, most often fights with siblings, and normal developmental forgetfulness and disorganisation with respect to jobs around the house, homework and her bedroom (which often looks as if the SAS has been training in it).

At this age, she has progressed from fairly black-and-white childhood thinking towards logical thought, and has a limited ability to extend logic to more 'grey' ideas, such as moral dilemmas. As her awareness of the way the world works increases, she easily gets anxious about all the possible bad things that may happen to her friends and family. She still has difficulty identifying how her immediate behaviour impacts upon her future. She scorns the imaginative and illogical thinking of her early childhood, but spends much time and energy accumulating general knowledge, and she has developed an ability to apply learned concepts to new tasks. She still likes to play games on her iPad, but increasingly uses the internet and social media to complete homework and chat with friends.

While still fairly self-absorbed, the early adolescent is slowly developing a conscience, moving from a 'what's in it for me?' approach to a desire to be well-liked by friends and live up to the expectations of people close to her (for example, she may place the needs of others over her own self-interest). Sadly, this new perspective is not always reflected in her behaviour, as can be seen from the emotionally charged conflicts ('relational aggression', as psychologists call it) that she and her friends engage in at school.

Main psychological need

At this age, the biggest question is: 'Am I normal?' This is when you'll notice your child beginning to spend a lot more time in front of the mirror and comparing herself to others. Adolescents are very sensitive to teasing about their appearance, so *never* tease or criticise your daughter about her body shape or weight. Help her, instead, to focus on developing a sense of mastery and accomplishment so she learns to see herself as a capable human being. (See 'Help her find her spark' on page 97).

MIDDLE ADOLESCENCE

In middle adolescence (14–17 years) girls are more independent and able to get themselves around and, as a result, there is less adult presence and protection in their lives.

The middle adolescent wants to be as grown up as possible. Mobile phones, social media and the internet; streamed TV series and music; and raunchy pop singers and glamorous celebrities have replaced her childhood icons. She uses the internet for study, but is often distracted by checking her Instagram feed and listening to new music on Spotify at the same time.

The emotional temperature in the home can rise as

tensions about matters such as spending time with family versus friends increase. Many young women at this age have friends who are drinking alcohol regularly or have dabbled in illicit drugs. Relationships have a very self-centred quality, which can be irritating to her parents, as is her ability to lose things. If her parents are not careful, she's likely to play them like a fiddle – this is especially important for parents to be aware of when there are two homes after separation or divorce.

The middle adolescent is in the process of developing new intellectual powers, such as thinking more about possibilities, and thinking more about the very process of thinking. She is thinking in multiple dimensions, and the ability to see in shades of grey increases. She does not always feel the need to waste precious minutes on thinking ahead or weighing up the consequences of her actions. She is particularly oversensitive to events, even more so than boys. Ordinary happenings often trigger strong emotions, and rejection by friends or romantic interests hurts more than at other ages due to this increased sensitivity.

Although she is still self-focused, the middle adolescent is increasingly concerned about what others, particularly her friends, think of her. Her need for peer group acceptance is so great that at school, and via social media at home after school and on weekends, she checks the 'popularity barometer' regularly. Gaining and keeping social approval is paramount. Her friendships still begin with things that she perceives as having in common with others, but increasingly involve the sharing of values and personal secrets. Being part of a friendship group provides her with a greater sense of security, though antisocial groups can increase risk-taking behaviours at this stage. Romantic crushes are common, as are dating and increased sexual activity. Her obsessive focus on peer friendships may also lead her to reject physical affection at home, which can be distressing for parents.

The middle adolescent has a growing desire for privacy and is sensitive about the changes her body continues to undergo. Her parents are noticing frequent mood swings, especially when she spends too much time alone. She tries to prove her individuality by spurning adult control and support, often resulting in more and more arguments. Her new thinking abilities may be shown in the use of sarcasm and in arguing with her parents and other authority figures, which may result in further clashes. She has greater interest in making her own decisions and benefits from more opportunities to do so (as long as they are things she is developmentally capable of doing).

The process of developing her own identity is intensifying and she is experimenting with different roles, looks, values and friendships, as well as her sexuality. Friendships help her explore and develop her identity. She is becoming surer of her own beliefs and may start making plans for her future. At the same time, body image may still be a central concern and her parents may be worried that her apparent low self-esteem may contribute to mental health problems, such as depression and eating disorders.

Main psychological need

For this age group, the big questions are 'Who am I?' and 'Where do I belong?' Teenagers at this stage are deeply concerned with self-discovery and can appear quite self-obsessed. Couple this with their emerging sexuality and the tendency for risk-taking behaviour and you can see how there's enormous potential for conflict in the home.

While they demand freedom, and fight to attain it, middle adolescents still need to feel that their parents are capable of taking care of them if life gets overwhelming. This is the classic adolescent paradox. They'll battle to dismantle your authority, but know that they can be undone if they are *too* successful. The more they feel themselves to be truly on their own and without parental support the more vulnerable they are, which may be particularly problematic if one or both parents are 'absent' due to divorce/separation or issues such as alcohol or drug abuse. However, even well-intentioned parents may feel that they start to check out when their middle adolescent shows signs of independence. You need to be a firm but loving mentor, not just a cashed-up housemate. See chapter 9 for more on encouraging mentors.

LATE ADOLESCENCE

Late adolescence refers to the years past high school, from around age 17 into the early 20s. By now she is physically an adult, and accepted as an adult in her environment. Many of her friends are seeking to pursue further education or work-related training. Her self-image is now more consistent with the realities of her size, shape and abilities. She has a well-established sexual identity, and has the capacity to engage in satisfying intimate relationships.

Despite her adult appearance, her brain is not fully developed (whatever she might think). She still needs help in linking effort to outcome, and with planning and organising.

She is now much less self-centred and can see the bigger societal picture, including the possibility of valuing moral principles over laws. On the other hand, her differing rates of cognitive and emotional development may mean she will argue for specific values and violate them at the same time. Her increased ability to empathise with others may mean more intense relationships and a tendency to worry more, with an almost obsessive concern for family and friends, and life problems.

Her parents are relieved to see that she is generally acting more responsibly. There are fewer conflicts with her parents nowadays and she is beginning to see them as individuals and take their perspectives into account. She is showing interest in taking on adult responsibilities, such as part-time work, having her own bank account and doing her own laundry.

Main psychological need

The key question in this phase is, 'Where am I going?' To answer this, an adolescent needs to have a strong sense of self that incorporates a realistic body image and an acceptance of gender identity and sexual orientation. With a strong sense of self, she can begin to develop mutually caring and responsible relationships and to form clear educational and vocational goals. The greatest protective factor against kids going off the rails is having a charismatic adult in their lives, someone they can talk to and from whom they can draw strength. For many adolescents this charismatic adult is a parent, but for others it might be a coach, a teacher, an uncle or aunt, a grandparent or a spiritual leader. (See page 99 for more on widening the circle of care around your daughter.)

RITES OF PASSAGE

In the grey zone between childhood and adulthood, the adolescent girl is caught between the past and the future. Although biologically mature, in that she is capable of sexual reproduction, she is still neither psychologically or socially mature. This has not always been the case. The notion of adolescence being a distinct developmental process is a relatively new phenomenon in Western societies – a by-product of the Industrial Revolution. What once was a gap of between two and four years from puberty to the adoption of adult roles (defined by work, marriage and parenthood) is now often well over a decade, thanks to increased wealth, longer periods in education and training, and a longer life span.

In some cultures there is a formal age of maturity, when young people are deemed to become adults. For example, initiation ceremonies that indicate the 'rite of passage' from child to adult are held by some Aboriginal Australians for children aged between 10 and 16. In the Jewish tradition, females are considered to be adult members of the community at age 12, and this transition is celebrated in the Bat Mitzvah (the Bar Mitzvah, the equivalent ceremony for boys, is held at age 13). In parts of Central and South America, celebrations known as quinceañeras mark a girl's 15th birthday. The celebration recognises the transition to womanhood, and dates back many centuries.

In mainstream Australia, events such as debutante balls, once designed to showcase young women to bachelors looking for the 'perfect bride', are still held in many schools. Today, debutante balls are characterised by the use of stretch limousines, boys in suits and coiffed, frocked-up, fake-tanned girls in virginal white, teetering on sparkly stilettos. Some institutions are changing the practice to ensure it reflects modern values; for example, by opening the event to same-sex couples. Other schools have ditched formalities due to fears of alcohol-related incidents and are substituting a simple and more rewarding end-of-year event, such as a four-day wilderness hike followed by a party with family and friends.

I believe there is much to be recommended in more formal rite-of-passage traditions. Without a ritual that says, 'Now you are an adult', the rapid biological changes of puberty can result in confusion, uncertainty and 'status anxiety'. In Australia, schoolies week seems to have become the default rite of passage for many young people at the end of their last school year, with thousands heading for coastal towns to celebrate the end of their exams and the beginning of their newfound freedom. Unfortunately, excessive use of alcohol and other drugs seems to have become an indispensable component of the festivities.

Chapter 4

Pressures at home

Up until now the teenage girl has largely been an extension of her parents, but during adolescence she begins to recognise her uniqueness and, above all, her separateness from them. She starts to develop her own set of values and morals. Ideally, during the early stages of moral development, parents provide their offspring with a structured set of rules about what is right and wrong, what is acceptable and unacceptable – in essence, a moral compass. In fact, it's important to understand that parents still play a critical role in the teenage years when it comes to the development of more adult constructs, such as morals and values.

Research indicates that family closeness is the most important factor associated with avoiding risk-taking behaviours such as the use of alcohol and other drugs, and suicidal behaviours. So while it seems that peer relationships are the most important thing to your teen-ager, it does *not* mean that parents are less important to them. Positive peer and family relationships both play key roles in healthy development – one does not replace the other.

A really useful goal for parents at this delicate developmental time is to try to spend at least 10 minutes a day in one-to-one, face-to-face conversation. This is where the adult turns off their phone, makes eye contact and demonstrates an interest in all aspects of their daughter's life by asking questions about friends, school and other islands of competence and focusing on their content and using reflective listening – paraphrasing back to them what they have said. This way she'll know a) that you are actually interested in her, b) you are actively listening to her and c) you have understood. It's simple but effective.

THE NEEDY PARENT

The extent to which parents know themselves will help or hinder the developmental process for adolescent girls. If a parent has a weak sense of his or her own identity, the teenager is likely to experience confusion and look to external sources for stronger signals of an acceptable identity. If she sees her emerging values, morals and beliefs as not matching her parents' 'ancient' versions, she restructures her beliefs into her own personal set. The pressure to rebel can sometimes be overwhelming, potentially making this a time of inner turmoil and all-out conflict. It can be a total transformation.

While this may be difficult for parents, this growing sense of a teenage girl's independent identity is a very positive and healthy transition. It is most difficult when parents, often mothers, have structured their relationship with their daughters around a friendship, rather than a parent–daughter relationship with all the associated parental responsibilities. There are many pitfalls to being your child's friend rather than their parent (I call this 'Lindsay Lohan parenting'). More on this in chapter 8.

CHANGING FAMILIES

The image of the typical Australian family as a mum and dad, two kids and the family dog has undergone a number of changes in recent decades. Since the 1970s, couple relationships have become much more fluid, with a strong emphasis on the individual, a consequent loss of connectedness and a trend away from marriage towards de facto relationships. De facto relationships are increasingly common for younger couples but are more likely to end in separation. There has also been a rise in OINK (One Income No Kids) and DINK (Dual Income No Kids) households, a percentage of which may have little or no involvement with young people and so indirectly contribute to the falling number of potential mentors for young people who lack access to adult guidance.

As it has elsewhere in the world, direct contact with extended families that traditionally sustained and nurtured Australians has decreased, with the result that many parents no longer have access to the wisdom and support of parents, grandparents and other extended family. Marriage is occurring later and is less likely to be for life, with a greater number of births happening outside of marriage. While divorce rates are decreasing and are more likely to occur at a later age (in part due to later marriages), around half still involve families with young children.

While adults often handle the physical and psychological fallout of separation and divorce with the best intentions, many struggle. Children are often deeply affected, at least in the short term. One in five Australian families are headed by a single parent, whether as a result of divorce, choice or due to other circumstances. While many children of single parents do very well, research suggests that outcomes for young people, such as mental wellbeing and academic achievement, are poorer, often as a result of less income in comparison to two-parent families.

In 2016, the Australian Institute of Family Studies published data drawn from the Longitudinal Study of Australian Children (involving 8000 children from all states and territories), which found that 43 per cent of those under the age of 13 have, at some point, lived in a non-traditional (i.e. not 'nuclear') household. This is due to higher divorce rates, less-stable de facto relationships, children being raised by separated parents in 'double-family' living arrangements, and multiple generations living together.

A corollary of this is that older children in such families may be less likely to have contact with the parent they no longer live with, i.e. the 'non-resident' parent (most likely their father). Other research shows that at least half of 10–17-year-olds in separated families move between two homes at least monthly, but around one-quarter of children aged 10–17 years see their non-resident parent less than once a year, or never. Add lashings of parental guilt to the problem of 'fractured families', and many parents seek to make it up to their children by indulging them. They become hesitant to use language that reflects their values or to set limits, which are basic principles of good parenting. Parents who are in conflict post-separation may also become locked in a popularity contest, leaving their offspring with no moral compass – instead indulging in laissez-faire parenting, where all the child's basic needs are met instantly but there is little love, guidance or wisdom provided (see chapter 8 for more about this).

In homes where young people are left to make the decisions that parents once did, a critical piece of development at this age goes missing. Although it sounds contradictory, teenagers actually *need* boundaries – it gives them a sense of security as well as something to rebel against in their quest to work out identity and purpose.

So work out what the boundaries are, and apply them consistently. Let your daughter use you as her excuse in the face of peer-group pressure – she can blame you for the 'no technology after 9 p.m.' rule when her friends want to exchange Instagram messages at midnight. While they may not always like it in the short term, your teenage daughter may well thank you later in life – but don't bet your house on it!

UNDER-FATHERING

With few exceptions a girl's attachment to her mother is far stronger than that with her father, which is why she must be far more negative in order to deny the strength of that bond. This explains the extreme conflict that can occur between mothers and daughters and why teenage girls are generally able to maintain closer connections to their fathers. However, many girls today lack good male role models in their daily lives. Fathers may be absent, not often present, or simply unavailable emotionally as a result of family breakdown or because their lives are focused on their careers and/or other ambitions. In some cases, long work hours have taken over from many traditional social, family and leisure activities.

Fathers are important in a girl's life. A father's unconditional love says to a girl that she is valued for more than the way she looks or the marks she gets at school. This support is particularly important once 'daddy's little girl' takes on the role of sullen teenager. Girls in conflict with their mothers and who have absent or hands-off fathers may come to rely on alternative, often distorted, models of masculinity that abound in the media and popular culture. They may believe, among other things, that men have difficulty expressing their feelings, are concerned with power and status, are homophobic, anti-authoritarian, and treat sex as a sport.

Fathers are the pivotal template on which daughters base many of their attitudes, values and beliefs about men. There are three areas in which fathers typically have an equal or greater effect on their daughters' lives than their mothers: creating a loving and trusting relationship with a male; expressing anger comfortably and appropriately (especially towards men); and dealing well with people in authority (being self-confident and self-reliant). It is important for fathers to think about ways that they can play their role in building their daughters' skills in these areas.

Chapter 5
Pressures at school

As we have seen, Princess B is in the process of establishing herself as an independent individual, while at the same time cementing her own social relationships. In addition to a sudden spurt in physical growth, adolescent girls are able to think more broadly and deeply about 18 months earlier than their male peers. (Most women reading this already knew that!) Thinking about *more* things is a normal part of the maturing process, but a mature girl understands her social world with a new level of awareness.

For the vast majority of adolescent girls, school is the daily setting for peer group face-to-face interaction. This is where they consolidate what they have learned at home about relationships, such as how to value another person's perspective, how to compromise and negotiate, and how to control aggressive impulses.

Although friendships are not, of course, unique to adolescence, they hit a peak of importance during the early and middle stages. If it seems at times that her friends are more important to her than you are, that she can talk more easily to her schoolmates or her schoolmate's mum than you, it's because her friends give her a sense of identity and help her along the path to independence. Thus friendships are pivotal in that the peer group can act as a 'psychological anchor' while she is separating from the old ties. Positive and supportive friends (psychologists call this a 'pro-social' peer group) play a key role in helping teenage girls tackle developmental tasks on their way to adulthood. The truth is that having a rich repertoire of friends is like having a mobile personal support group that simultaneously provides a sense of meaning, purpose and belonging.

The degree to which girls feel part of an accepting peer group is also a major indicator of how well they will develop in other social and psychological spheres across adolescence and into adulthood. Research indicates, for example, that adolescents who are accepted by their peers and have mutually supportive friendships achieve better academic results and have a more positive self-image than those who don't. Research with adults reinforces these findings; those who had interpersonal problems in adolescence are at much greater risk of psychosocial difficulties in adulthood.

Within the security of a pro-social peer group, girls are likely to experience being valued and listened to. But they can also feel a sense of security and comfort in being with others who are experiencing the same developmental challenges, such as puberty and menstruation. Identity formation is assisted because the peer group is the perfect vehicle to experiment with different values, roles and identities. It is also a chance to test out early romantic and sexual relationships.

The key message is that who your daughter hangs out with matters big time, so take an interest in her peers, without being too nosy (a fine line). While our girls were younger it was quite easy to play social secretary, but by the time they are 16, in almost all cases you will have been fired from that job.

THE CLIQUE

Peer groups in adolescence are often referred to as cliques – basically groups of young people bonded through shared interests or characteristics. At school, these groups are mostly about who has power and who doesn't, who's in and who's out, who's cool and who's not. Of course, every school is different and some cohorts are amazingly civilised and develop a very positive ethos as a result of the particular mix of students in any single year. What type of cohort your daughter gets is an important life lottery, over which parents have limited control.

Often parents are unaware of how their daughters are treated at school or how they treat others, as some girls construct a social bubble around themselves as part of the process of becoming independent from parents. As a result, parents may be unaware of the nature and extent of their personal relationships until something untoward happens.

Books such as *Queen Bees and Wannabes*, films such as *Mean Girls* and the TV series *Gossip Girl* portray cliques very well. Depending on a girl's personality, temperament and emotional maturity, a clique can exert a major influence on who she does or does not talk to, which subjects she chooses, what after-school activities she engages in, how she wears her hair, and her values and beliefs. It can, in large part, determine her sense of self. For this reason, providing as it does a sort of second family, the clique can weaken the parent–daughter bond, and is likely to be where girls turn when in trouble.

Cliques also have a bearing on girls' relationships with boys. Having a boyfriend increases a girl's sense of self-worth and her status with her peers, although some girls will, in order to please a partner, sacrifice their friendships with their friends.

The relationships within such a group are sophisticated and multilayered, and every member comes to know and understand that her position is unstable and may change at any time. Ask the staff at any girls' school across Australia, and you'll discover that most year levels have at least two alpha females who vie for power. Alpha females also exist in co-educational schools and in both instances are best thought of as the social conductors; non-alpha females are her orchestra. And it is these girls who more often than not become Princess Bitchface at home, since the techniques they use to manipulate family members are the same ones they use to control friends.

The alpha female almost always has good looks and charisma, loves being the centre of attention, can be very assertive, and has an almost hypnotic power over others in the clique. She seeks to weaken any potentially threatening alliances/friendships in order to strengthen her own power and influence. She will ignore and exclude anyone she does not deem worthy of being in her group. She will often seek to destabilise peers by being nice to them one day and unpleasant the next, so that they never know where they stand. Another technique is to be particularly nice to one person as a means of pitting her against or snubbing another. Despite all these character-istics, she often slips under the adult radar and may be seen by adults as clever and charming.

> After a year at secondary school, Ella's new best friend was Amelia, who was more mature and sophisticated and had become the single biggest influence in Ella's life. Amelia was the leader of the Cool Group, whose members were everything Ella wanted to be, but wasn't. Ella soon dumped her primary school friends, remade her look and began smoking cigarettes, going to elaborate lengths to hide this from her non-smoking parents.

A clear picture of how this story could end is dramati-cally portrayed in the 2003 movie *Thirteen* – a must-see for any parent! In the film, 13-year-old Tracy starts middle school as a bright but relatively innocent young woman. Tracy feels that her mother, Melanie, is too preoccupied with her boyfriend to address her increasing depression. After being tormented about her choice of clothes, Tracy opts to shed her 'little girl' image by having her mother buy her cooler clothes. Alpha-girl classmate Evie praises Tracy's clothes and asks her to go shopping with her and her friend Astrid. Tracy gets caught up in a shopping spree using money from a stolen wallet, and Tracy and Evie end up fast friends. Evie introduces Tracy to her world of sex, drugs, self-harm and criminal activity, and while Melanie is increasingly concerned, she has trouble finding a way to intervene. Tracy and Evie become increasingly close and out of control, and Tracy shuts Melanie further out of her life. Eventually, Tracy starts to realise the negative effects of her lifestyle, but has to face a further challenge when Evie's legal guardian accuses her, not Evie, of being the bad influence. Without giving away the ending, suffice to say that the journey taken by Melanie and Tracy is rapid, devastating and all too believable.

COVERT AGGRESSION

A feature of interactions between adolescent girls is that any aggression is expressed covertly, or 'undercover'. While boys may act out hostile feelings and even come to blows, it is over quickly and usually that is the end of the matter. Girls are a different story – outright aggression is still considered largely unacceptable. The letters I receive at my magazine column suggest a commonly held view that expressing rage directly can result in the loss of relationships with others, and the prospect of isolation terrifies girls. There is an inbuilt conflict between their feelings of anger towards their peers and their adopted societal role as caretakers obliged to sacrifice their own needs for others. So they rely more heavily on psychological devastation – dirty looks, cyber bullying, taunting notes and ostracism. 'Cool' girls have lots of friends and typically don't involve themselves in direct conflict.

The fear of confrontation makes anger a circular issue that increases the scope of the conflict and causes girls to use relationships as weapons. Although the weak will more often be preyed upon, this sort of 'relational aggression' (the psychological term) is less about external characteristics and more often to do with conflict that has not been addressed directly and openly. In other words, girls tend not to get closure on the conflict because they don't have the opportunity to express their anger in a healthy, fulfilling way. They must be 'friends', superficially at least, with everyone. As a result, resentments often linger. This leads to grudges and, in some cases, future acts of vengeance. At home, the intensity of conflicts with parents can often be the result of the pent-up frustration that adolescent girls feel at school.

Alexandra had three children who loved life and everything it had to offer. Her eldest, Zara, had never given her any cause for concern; she'd been school captain at her primary school and was popular, smart and well regarded by friends and family. When she entered high school, Alex felt Zara start to drift away from her. Their communication was less frequent, her daughter's behaviour more secretive, and social media and friends became the centre of Zara's life. Yet Alex wasn't worried as Zara's grades remained high and she seemed to be involved in a plethora of school activities including sport, music, dance and drama. Instagram and Snapchat had become an electronic camp fire that Zara and her friends huddled around (albeit virtually) every night. Alex's own friends told her that this was normal teenage behaviour. So it was a massive shock when the school called her in to discuss a serious allegation of cyber bullying that had been made against her daughter. As the principal of the school solemnly handed her transcripts of a vile tirade using the foulest language written by Zara and aimed at some unfortunate peer, Alex went numb with disbelief. The school counsellor explained that Zara was the leader of a popular clique of girls, and had instructed them to turn on this one girl, who had subsequently attempted self-harm.

Alex's first reaction, apart from shock, was denial. To her it was simply inconceivable that her daughter even knew the meaning of such vile words, let alone had directed them at another person. When the principal explained that it was often hard for parents to believe that their child might be a bully, she felt herself becoming angry and defensive. But she knew she had to stay calm and concentrate on getting the facts. She asked for as much detail as was known about the frequency and extent of the bullying behaviour, and also what sanctions the school planned to impose. She thanked them for bringing the matter to her attention and told them that she would cooperate with the school to do everything she could to get this behaviour to stop. She asked the counsellor for advice on speaking to her daughter, and committed to staying in touch with Zara's year level coordinator and receiving feedback on her progress.

If you have a girl at the top of the heap who has behaved like Zara, don't feel guilty. She's not necessarily a bad person and you're not a bad parent, but it *is* your job to point out what is going on and how it can impact on others. And don't forget that those in a position of privilege don't like to be told they should change, nor do they believe that there really is a problem. Affirm her, but hold her accountable: 'I love you, but I don't love your behaviour.'

Also, be aware (but not pre-emptively alarmed) that being in the top clique can mean your daughter is vulnerable to health-compromising behaviours such as early sexual activity and drug use. Bear in mind, too, that she no doubt knows this sort of life is a house of cards, which may cause anxiety and, indeed, may fuel her negative behaviour.

While it is tempting to minimise or dismiss this behaviour as a phase, or find other excuses ('It's probably the other girl's fault' or 'She's under a lot of pressure at school', etc.), parents must take bullying very seriously. Research shows that bullying can have extremely serious consequences for the victim in the short, medium and long term. These can include anxiety, poor self-esteem, depression, refusing to attend school and even suicidal thoughts and self-harm.

In a case like Zara's, her mother must explain the seriousness of these allegations to her daughter. Aside from tarnishing Zara's reputation, her place at school could be in jeopardy and in these litigious days, legal action could be taken against her. Alex should calmly explain precisely what the school has said and give Zara the opportunity to respond. Zara needs to hear that whatever transpired, everyone makes poor choices, and that her mother is going to help her get through this.

Alex needs to avoid going into lecture mode or finger-wagging. While there is merit in having a discussion to discover if Zara is upset, jealous, unhappy or perhaps has been subjected to harassment herself, what is also needed is a simple declaration that no matter what the circumstances, bullying and harassment are unacceptable, and must stop. (See chapter 12 for more on bullying.)

ACADEMIC PRESSURE

In later primary school and early secondary school years, the curriculum frequently includes more abstract, demanding material. Since not all adolescent girls develop formal thought processes at the same rate, this may be frustrating for Princess B. In addition, she must expand her verbal skills to cope with these more complex ideas and tasks, not only at school but also as she prepares for life as an adult. The limited language of childhood is no longer adequate. Some early adolescents may appear less competent than their peers because of a lack of ability to express themselves meaningfully.

In middle adolescence your daughter is expected to start to develop vocational goals. As part of the process of establishing her own identity, she is often asked to focus on the question, 'What do you plan to be when you grow up?' This is to identify, at least at a preliminary level, what she wants to do and how she intends to achieve it. Given what we now know about brain development, this is both premature and unfair.

My daughter started Year 11 this year and I don't think
she is coping very well. She insists everything is fine
when I ask her (she actually gets quite frustrated and
angry when I do), but her grades have gone right down
and her teachers report that she is quite disruptive in
class. I'm worried that she's going to bomb out and end
up working in a supermarket for half her life like I did.
What can I do?

The reality is that some girls lack the emotional and
psychological maturity to do the final years of school. The
solution can be a gap year between Year 11 and Year 12,
which allows her time to mature. Often this involves either
some overseas travel, volunteer work or getting a full-time
job in a relatively menial role. The key for parents (especially in the case of an established pattern of behaviour) is
to explore systematically what lies behind the disruptive
behaviour and being especially vigilant for the symptoms
of specific psychological problems such as anxiety or
depression as well as the presence of learning difficulties
or disabilities. Any decision needs to be made in conjunc-
tion with the school, who often have more objectivity than
parents. Another option is to spread the final year over a
couple of years to make the task somewhat easier.

CONFLICT WITH AUTHORITY

Problems can also arise at school around this time when
teachers and other staff forget that young women tend to
become very sensitive to control, and conflict with authority figures at school is not uncommon. As the teenage girl

pushes for increased autonomy and independence, there may be conflict over issues at school such as obeying school rules, uniform and grooming requirements. What may seem like a small issue to an adult (e.g. having to wear sensible black or brown shoes as part of the school uniform) can be considered a huge deal for a teenage girl, especially if she is experiencing it for the first time. Princess B thrives on conflict and will often seek it out or actively manufacture it. She loves a drama – even more so if it is one of her own making.

Conflict, however, is not necessarily a negative thing – when managed well, it is a useful tool. It is, after all, the process through which people confront and resolve their differences. So conflict should not come as a shock; it should be expected.

> Petula has had a wonderful holiday with her family in Bali, and while there she and a friend decided to experiment with a different hair colour. She has returned home with neon green hair and red tips. Despite her mum suggesting that she return to her previous lustrous brunette colouring before going back to school, Petula decided to begin term 4 at her private school with her new look. The school rather predictably sent her home, demanding that she change her hair colour and obey the school rules.

If your daughter is in conflict with the school over a uniform breach, use it as an opportunity to teach her about rules and regulations. Explain that when you enrolled your child in the school you essentially signed a contract on her behalf that stated the need for her to comply with the expectations of the school. This is a good life lesson. If she does not want to obey these rules, then that is her choice, but she will have to bid farewell to her friends and attend a school that has no hair-colour restrictions.

Chapter 6

Pressures in cyberspace

This is the most 'tribal' generation Australia has ever seen, in that they have access to each other 24/7 via mobile phones, apps and the internet. Previous generations had to limit their socialising to the (shared) family phone, or wait until they got to school or the weekend came around. These days, your daughter's friends become a 'second family' at a much younger age than in generations before. Digital technology has also given today's adolescents much more privacy, as communication with others can take place out of earshot, and often out of sight, of their parents. Both of these factors serve to not only weaken the traditional parent–child connection, but also leave many parents completely in the dark about what is happening in their children's lives. The lack of parental awareness at increasingly younger ages can lead to devastating consequences, seen most tragically in cases where young women have committed suicide in response to cyber bullying that their parents knew nothing about.

Your daughter's technological world is the single

biggest difference between your teenage years and her teenage years. While being online for hours on end may seem foreign to you, your daughter doesn't differentiate between online and offline worlds – it's all one world. And in general terms, young people use the internet and social media for many positive reasons, such as keeping in touch with friends and family, finding and sharing information, supporting friends and reaching out via social networks to others who are experiencing similar problems.

While we know that the majority of teenagers use social networking services, there is also an increase in the use of other online forums, including wikis (Wikipedia and WikiHow) and blogging sites (Blogger and WordPress). Facebook remains popular, but its use by teenagers has decreased significantly, from 70 per cent in 2012 to 58 per cent in 2013 – frankly, they don't want to be hanging out in the same e-space as their parents or grandparents. Other popular social media sites at the time of writing include YouTube, Instagram, Snapchat and Tumblr. Increasingly, access to the internet is via smartphone. Australian research indicates that almost 90 per cent of teenagers aged 14–17 have a mobile phone and, of these, almost three-quarters have a smartphone. The number of teenagers using a mobile phone to access the internet tripled between 2009 and 2013.

THE BAD NEWS

A survey conducted in 2015 by Plan Australia and Our Watch (the national anti-violence against women organisation) asked 600 teenage girls about their experiences online. Almost three-quarters reported that they were often bullied and harassed online. Both this study and other Australian research shows us that around half of secondary school students have sent and/or received a sexually explicit text message, and around one quarter have sent a sexually explicit nude or nearly nude photo or video of themselves. This increases to 50 per cent if the young person is already sexually active. In contrast to this, 4 out of 5 students in the Plan Australia survey said it was unacceptable for a boyfriend to ask for a naked photo, and almost half said they felt much less prepared to tackle online harassment and bullying online compared to offline, in spite of recent public and school-based campaigns. It seems that young women feel they have to comply, even though they don't necessarily want to.

In the hands of most teenagers, social media platforms are relatively benign, fun places to share photos with friends, and chances are they will remain just a normal part of their world. Most teenagers avoid the screen-induced self-loathing that arises from social networking and gain a small self-esteem boost in viewing their own profiles. As outlined above, they will have a strong enough emerging personal identity that they won't need external point-scoring to feel good about themselves.

But in the hands of Princess B, with her immature brain, vanity and insatiable desire for retaliation and vengeance, a social media site such as Instagram becomes a multi-headed 'frenemy'. It not only becomes another tool for confirming her self-obsessed tendencies, it can also be a seething hotbed of bitter envy and resentment.

Instagram shows status and emotions in a way that other tools like Facebook status updates simply can't. It is pure, unadulterated, optical grandstanding, where energy, excitement, beauty and wealth are captured in a single photograph. Instagram has become a digital Colosseum – a home to what has become a gladiatorial battle of the selfies.

So if your daughter is asking for an Instagram or other social media account, hold off for as long as you can, especially if she is already showing the Princess B tendencies described – she doesn't need it. If she has one already, note the way she monitors and reacts to the perceived presence or absence of enough 'likes' on a selfie. It will be a sign about what's important to her, and what may need to be done to rebalance the influences on her emerging identity. If she is devastated by few likes, engage her in 'spark' activities (see page 97) and offline friendships as often as you can. And spend uninterrupted time just listening to her.

THE GOOD NEWS

The good news is that young people are pretty savvy when it comes to privacy and protecting their digital reputation. Research conducted by the Young and Well Cooperative Research Centre in 2012 indicated that the vast majority of young people use privacy settings online and limit what certain friends or community members can see. Contrary to media reports, the research showed that 81 per cent decided not to post something online as they were worried that it may reflect badly on them in future years.

Furthermore, three-quarters of young people had taken proactive steps to limit the amount of information available online and over half had tried to remove content posted online. The research also demonstrated that many young people were cool in a crisis, with 33 per cent seeking advice about what to do when they came across mean or cruel behaviour online. Thirty per cent had reported a person's behaviour or an incident online and 10 per cent had reported a person or incident to an authority, either teachers or police.

In other good news, research shows that there are actually many benefits associated with using social media – a side of the story we rarely hear about. The benefits include helping to facilitate supportive relationships, identity formation and increased feelings of belonging and self-esteem – all factors that protect young people against negative outcomes. In fact, promoting internet and media literacy can actually *help* young people deal with risks such as cyber bullying and predation.

Chapter 7

Princess B in action

Adolescents, in their quest for emotional and psychological independence, can feel torn between their yearning to stay close to their families (the safety and security of childhood) and their strong drive to spend every waking moment away from them (the rise of the peer group). Every adolescent deals with this separation differently, though bouts of uncooperative or even hostile behaviour are fairly standard.

Some adolescent girls, however, become stuck in a groove of conflict with everything and everyone in their orbit. This can result in a three- to five-year period of psychological warfare that can be frightening in its intensity. In the most extreme cases the family finds itself living with a girl on the edge, whose 'rebellion in over-drive' fuels a pattern of self-destructive behaviour – an emotionally starved young woman who knows only *that* she needs, without understanding *what* she needs. For Princess B, the more vulnerable she feels, the more aggressive her physical and verbal behaviour tends to become. At worst, she will keep up a snide commentary targeting her parents, and in the process she will suss out their most sensitive buttons and press them over and over again.

More often than not the clash is greatest between daughters and mothers. Chalk and cheese are the principal ingredients of this conflict – mother and daughter, once so close, suddenly find themselves on different planets. The mother is trying desperately to talk to her clearly distressed daughter, while the daughter rejects or ignores such overtures as if they are intrusive telemarketing calls.

There is some comfort for parents trying to cope with this phase, in that all this adolescent rebellion is actually – as we have seen – a *normal developmental process*. Despite the disturbance that families characteristically live through in the teenage years, most young people eventually adopt the values of their parents. When they finally do so, experience shows that a more whole-hearted acceptance usually occurs than would have been the case if they had not challenged those views in the first place.

I want to look now at some of the behaviours of Princess B, and some of the negative thinking patterns that underlie them. I should preface this by saying that while all adolescent girls will engage in this type of thinking and behaviour at times, for Princess B these become her default settings. Now this may sound harsh, but unless parents are prepared to acknowledge that Princess B's behaviour is abnormal, they cannot take steps to deal with it, which is what I talk about in Part 2.

CHALLENGING BEHAVIOURS

While it's entirely normal for most teenage girls to view their adult carers as embarrassing, and to be mildly dismissive or avoidant of them, Princess B will develop an ongoing pattern of manipulative, rude behaviour. This is combined with an inability to tolerate criticism, along with a chronic tendency to belittle and disparage others in an attempt to validate her feelings of superiority. It is important to stress how such a cocooned, spoilt and entitled individual can emerge from a loving and well-intentioned family. Princess B exhibits a decreased ability to accept responsibility for her actions, while her parents, in a desperate attempt to avoid conflict and confrontation, become more indulgent in response. It is the initial anaemic response from her adult carers that feeds and enables this monstrous behaviour. In order to reduce the likelihood of this occurring, parents need to be aware of the many and varied ploys that Princess B uses to manipulate her family.

The damsel in distress

This involves acting helpless and dependent, so parents feel sympathetic and end up doing things for them – from homework assignments to transportation. Princess B effectively teaches her parents not to expect a whole lot from her, and may keep it up until she's had an apartment and car bought for her.

> Sasha is in Year 9. Her history teacher set a term-long project on Ancient Greece and suggested ways in which the students could manage their time so that they could

finish the project by the end of the term. It's now the last week of term, and Sasha is in her bedroom crying inconsolably because she has too much work left to do on the project. Her mother, seeing that all Sasha has completed so far is a very nicely coloured-in front page, starts to google useful references and jot down notes.

While Sasha's distress is likely to be genuine, her mother is contributing to the problem by rescuing her daughter from the consequences of her actions. The best approach would be to resist the overwhelming desire to say 'I told you so', remain calm, acknowledge her feelings ('I can see you are really upset about this') and then offer to help her draw up a time-management plan for the final week of term. Her mother needs to affirm that she trusts in Sasha's abilities ('I know you can do this') and then leave her to it. Under no circumstances should Mum accede to Sasha's demands that a) her mother write a note to the school along the lines of 'the dog ate my homework' or b) do her homework for her or c) resort to a bribe. It is vital that Sasha experiences the consequences of her poor choices and lack of planning and organisation. Standing one's ground will, of course, result in sulking, tantrums, threats and insults – but the cost of caving in is stratospherically higher in the long run.

The chore dodger

Princess B will simply refuse to do household jobs and will either put on a floorshow of petulant outrage or alternatively present her parents with a long list of excuses

('I've got too much homework', 'I'm studying for an exam', 'So-and-so never has to do this', etc.). Alternatively, she will simply organise her life so that she is conveniently absent when she knows it is time to do things such as the dishes or cleaning up.

Princess B is not alone. A comparison of time-use surveys shows us that Australian teenagers' overall contribution to household work is small and getting smaller. The average time girls spent doing household tasks was 28 minutes per day in 2006, compared to 40 minutes per day in 1992. While 5.6 per cent of teenage girls did no housework at all in 1996, this rose to nearly 16 per cent in 2006. Researchers also noted that increasing gender equality plays out in a different way than expected in terms of teenagers' contribution to housework. Girls have become more 'domestically useless' like their brothers, rather than boys doing more.

So how should you deal with a chore dodger? Some parents wave the white flag when it comes to chores, despairing of ever getting their daughters to pick up after themselves or help around the house. Others mount a crusade of constant aggression with lots of demands, threats and bellowing. Neither approach is likely to help things much. The truth is that creating a *mildly* sloppy teen is possible. It involves forethought and consistency on the part of the adult carer, and some changes in behaviour and expectations. But done right, the pay-off is big: a better relationship with your teenager and a cleaner home. The secret lies in making a connection between adult freedom and adult responsibility. That's the exchange. Parents need to respect Princess B's need for independence and individuality by allowing her, say, to choose how she dresses, or what posters she puts on the walls in her room, while ensuring that she has some respect for their ground rules. Allowing your teenage daughter more self-expression and self-determination makes it easier to agree on chores. So what to do?

1. Choose your battleground and decide what's really essential to you and what you're willing to let slide.
2. Come to an agreement. Come up with a chore plan that both parent and teenager are comfortable with.
3. Be absolutely clear. Don't make the mistake of assuming that she will know what you mean when you say 'clean up your room'. Be specific. Does it involve clearing out rubbish and dirty dishes? Putting away clean clothing? Taking dirty washing to the laundry? Vacuuming? Dusting?
4. Discuss sensible consequences if she doesn't stick to the agreement, e.g. earlier curfews, reduced internet or phone access, removal of car privileges.

What if she still doesn't lift a finger? Calmly explain to her that since she has chosen not to do the agreed chore, you'll hire someone to do it – and pay for it out of her pocket money.

The guilt inducer

This tactic is one of the oldest tricks in the book. Princess B, after being told no, wails that 'everybody else' has got a particular model of mobile phone or an iPad, or is allowed to go to the upcoming 18-and-over music festival or is allowed to drink at parties or is . . . [insert outrageous, inappropriate or ridiculous demand]. This is the time-honoured 'If you really loved me . . .' technique and often works with parents who are time-poor, recently separated or concerned with social status and keeping up appearances (i.e. if their daughter is the only one in her group without an iPhone, it reflects poorly on them).

Your response? 'I understand how hard it is to miss out, but the answer is no.' And when your daughter continues with guilt-induction by crying and at the same citing a long list of all the other things her friends can do or have, hold firm. 'It's interesting to hear how others deal with these situations. In our household, these are our rules.' Then walk AWAY!

The vulture

This is where Princess B, having carefully observed her parents' communication patterns for a while, decides who is the weaker parent and swoops in with a combination of charm, flattery and/or guile, to channel all requests through that particular adult. Once that naïve parent is hooked, Princess B uses his or her agreement to try to coerce cooperation from the other parent. This is also known as 'divide and conquer', and is a strategy that many daughters learn from a young age. If Princess B is still using it in the teen years, it's going to be a tough one to deal with for two reasons. Firstly, she's probably been using this technique successfully for over a decade, and secondly it suggests that there may be ongoing problems in parental unity. If this sounds like your family situation, it is important to talk to your partner about how you will deal with any such demand, particularly requests that involve financial or safety repercussions. My recommendation is to repeat, ad nauseam, 'I can't answer that until I talk to your father/mother.'

A particularly challenging version of this occurs in separated or divorced families. If conflict is high between separated parents, and Princess B spends some time with each parent in their respective households, she may well use this to her advantage. In these situations, trying to be on the same page may seem impossible. So if you are the parent who is setting boundaries and you feel that your ex-partner isn't, you may find it much harder to deal with Princess B's barrage of demands. Set up a time to sort it out with your ex-partner in a family dispute resolution session at one of the many family services throughout Australia or, if possible, communicate via email or text. If you have an existing parenting plan, it's worth looking at whether it needs updating to address how you will deal collaboratively with 'vulture' behaviour.

The ambit claimant

This involves Princess B making an absolutely outrageous request, which when refused results in feigned disbelief at how unreasonable, heritage-listed and inflexible her parents are being, accompanied by threats to abscond to Sweden, or to call the child abuse hotline. This exchange can last for days, raising the emotional temperature in the family to boiling point; then at the last moment, in an apparent conciliatory gesture, she suggests a compromise (which was the real goal from the start). It usually appears in the form of, 'Well if I can't do that, can I at least do this?' Parents are often so emotionally exhausted and battered by the debate that they often relent.

Unfortunately, if an adolescent is prepared to work this hard to get her way, it means this tactic has worked before. A teenager who pushes parents for days on end in this way knows only too well that they're going to crack. The best way to deal with such an onslaught of emotional manipulation is to resort to the 'broken record' technique, repeating your refusal. (The term refers to the tendency for old vinyl recordings that had been scratched to repeat one section over and over until you shifted the needle.) When Princess B is trying hard to persuade you, she often does not really hear your refusal. At best, she may see it as an objection that can be overcome by persistence. When the adult carer repeats the *same words*, the pattern-recognition ability of the brain eventually notices that something is being repeated and Princess B starts to take notice of what you are saying. When she realises she is bashing her head against a brick wall, she will eventually give up (with most people, this will be quite quickly).

The distracter

This technique involves choosing a moment when one or both parents are distracted or really busy (or have had a few drinks), and then asking permission for something specific. Often the parents aren't even fully aware of what they have given permission for. Princess B will then interpret this 'permission' as a metaphorical blank cheque to do almost anything, and then express righteous indignation if called to account.

To deal with this situation, it is best to admit that you weren't listening, but that you reserve the right to change your mind. It's also important to call her out on her behaviour: 'I think you were aware of the fact that we were busy talking with your sister/socialising with friends when you claim we gave permission. You were well aware that we were not focused on what you were asking, and took advantage of the situation.' Then exit stage left.

The debater

When confronted, or attempts are made to hold Princess B accountable for her choices, she often responds by attempting to drag her parents into a seemingly endless, emotionally draining and gruelling debate by deftly mounting an argument that changes the focus from her behaviour to theirs. Typically she will set off on a number of predictable pathways, where she may point out how inconsistent, imperfect and hypocritical her parents are; blame her friends or the parents of friends; or argue that the rules were different for siblings. When confronted with this technique, parents need to seize control and end the discussion by saying, 'I can see that you are upset, so we will talk about this after dinner.' Just make sure you give a time for the discussion and stick to it.

The blackmailer

This involves a pattern of issuing threats that Princess B knows will push her parents' buttons: 'I'll run away from home', 'I'll kill myself', 'I'll ring child protection services', and so on. Parents are so terrified that something drastic will happen that they invariably give in. This form of emotional blackmail is particularly powerful and distressing for everyone involved. It can occasionally also involve episodes of self-harm.

It can feel very scary when your daughter says she wants to kill herself or makes other threats, particularly if someone you love has completed suicide. In most instances daughters are trying to communicate something to the adults in their life, but more often than not, it isn't clear what that is. Commonly, she is simply using words she knows are powerful and attention-getting in order to underline her level of distress rather than to convey actual suicidal intent. Such threats are often said in anger or as a way to manipulate you. Three things lie behind such expressions of anger in teenage girls: hurt, fear or frustration. Acknowledging the underlying issue and addressing it is the desired outcome.

If this is a repeated pattern of behaviour, seek professional advice. Press an emotional pause button by saying something like, 'I would like us to talk to a professional about this', then take her to a GP and start the process of finding a psychologist, counsellor or other mental health expert.

The risk-taker

It's absolutely normal for teenage girls to crave new experiences – and this is one of the most nerve-racking and stressful aspects of being a parent. They do this to explore their own limits and abilities, to test the boundaries, and to express themselves as individuals. It's all part of their journey to becoming independent young adults, complete with their own identities. The problem, as mentioned earlier, is that the part of their brain that handles planning and impulse control doesn't mature until the early 20s. This means they are more likely than adults to make quick decisions without always thinking through the consequences. Sometimes teenagers will make decisions about engaging in potentially risky behaviours to fit in with a group, such as fighting, truancy, unprotected sexual activity, tobacco smoking, alcohol use, binge-drinking, illegal substance use, dangerous driving or illegal activities like graffiti, trespassing or vandalism. The difference between Princess B and other girls is the age of initiation and the intent, intensity and frequency of such behaviours.

Parents confronted with an acting-out, risk-taking daughter should try to remain calm. You might feel like sobbing, or doing a commendable imitation of Mount Vesuvius, but this is not about you – it's about your daughter, and she needs you to be the adult. Screaming at her may be cathartic in the short term, but it actually achieves nothing and may in fact result in an escalation of the behaviour and lead her to withdraw from prosocial peers, school and the family or worse [insert your most dreaded nightmare]. So in order not to exacerbate the situation, it is essential that the lines of communication be kept open.

In almost all cases, the risk-taking behaviour has a purpose and the young woman may be trying to communicate something, make a statement or punish herself, her adult carers or the family as a whole. The trick is to look behind the behaviour to see what is really going on. Does your daughter feel safe, valued and listened to? What pressures is she experiencing at school or in her peer group? Could she be anxious? Many of us have blinkers on when it comes to our daughters and we often lack objectivity, so encouraging her to talk to another trusted adult such as a school counsellor, family doctor or psychologist can be of enormous assistance. See later in the book for more on alcohol, drugs and mental health.

The abuser

There are some girls who exhibit a sustained pattern of oppositional, aggressive or violent behaviour that is so severely disruptive and distressing that it has been classified as a mental disorder. Intermittent explosive disorder (IED) is currently categorised in the *Diagnostic and Statistical Manual of Mental Disorders V* (DSM-5) under the 'Disruptive, Impulse-Control, and Conduct Disorders' category. It is diagnosed if there are recurrent outbursts that demonstrate an inability to control impulses.

The disorder itself is not easily diagnosed, as it often presents with other mood disorders, particularly bipolar disorder. Individuals diagnosed with IED report their outbursts as being brief (lasting less than an hour) and with a variety of bodily symptoms including sweating, stuttering, tightness in the chest, twitching and palpitations. Many say that they experience a sensation of relief (and in some cases pleasure) after they perform aggressive acts, but that these are later followed by remorse. Researchers have recently found IED to be nearly twice as common as previously thought. Importantly, it is a behavioural disorder that is a medical condition in the same way that depression or panic disorder is – it is not simply bad behaviour. If you suspect that your daughter's behaviour may be consistent with IED, then you should seek help from your GP or a mental health professional.

DISTORTED THINKING

As we have seen, adolescence can be a very stressful time for young people. This, combined with an immature brain, can make young people vulnerable to developing unhelpful thought processes. Some girls are prone to persistent negative thoughts about themselves or others, which lead to feelings of sadness, resentment, jealousy or anger, and they can become locked in a downward spiral. As a parent, you can't know what your child is thinking, but their behaviour can certainly give you plenty of clues.

There are many online tools and apps to help young people become aware of their self-talk. Type 'Brave Program' or 'Mood Gym' into a search engine, for example, and you will have free access to evidence-based, interactive, online programs for the prevention and treatment of adolescent anxiety and depression. The programs are free, and provide ways for teenagers to better cope with their moods and worries. These programs are particularly appealing to teenage girls because of their accessibility, confidentiality, convenience, anonymity and affordability. There are also programs available for parents.

Some of the most common distorted thought processes are described here.

All-or-nothing thinking

She thinks in absolutes – people, things or events are black or white, good or bad, with no middle ground. She tends to pronounce judgement using general labels: 'She's a slut', 'She's a loser' or 'He's a nerd'. She will condemn others on the basis of a single occasion or encounter.

> Carmel's parents were keen to have her broaden her interests, so they took her to a local dance studio to check out some of the classes on offer. She attended one class but then refused to return, saying that the school was 'retarded' and that she would never go back. Carmel was 14.

Rather than overreacting and yelling at her, Carmel's parents need to calmly point out that the use of the term 'retarded' is inappropriate, and that she needs to find other words to explain the source of her discontent. Identifying why she is unhappy in the class is critical to finding a solution that truly fits the situation. Is it the physical demands of the class? A potential mismatch of the teacher's and the student's personalities? The style of dance? Or is she feeling generally stressed, tired and over-scheduled, or is afraid of failing? Having a discussion to tease out what lies behind the words will often then lead parents to a solution. It is really about being a psychological Sherlock Holmes, a 'needs' detective.

Catastrophising

She tends to magnify and exaggerate the importance of events, anticipating how awful or unpleasant they will be. She constantly predicts that negative things will happen, always overestimating the chance of a disaster. If she does suffer a setback, she will view it as part of a never-ending pattern of defeat.

> Naomi, a Year 11 student, has an important test next week. Her parents know that she has studied hard for it, but Naomi is in a panic because she has convinced herself she will fail, that this will set the trend for both Year 11 and 12, and that she will probably die lonely and poor.

The solution to this type of thinking is threefold: the first step is to encourage the young woman to recognise and challenge this type of thinking. This is where programs like Mood Gym (mentioned earlier) are so useful. It can teach her to stop the inner critic quickly. Parents can teach their daughter that as soon as these thoughts pop up, she can inwardly shout, 'No!' or 'NOPE, we are not going down that path again!' This will disrupt that train of thought and help her to feel more level-headed again. Secondly, teach her to focus on her breathing.

After disrupting the thought, encourage her to be still for a minute or two. Sit her down if possible. Get her to focus on just her in-breaths and out-breaths. Nothing else. This will calm her body down, which helps her to think more clearly and to return to what is happening right now in this moment instead of being lost in future worries. Smart phone apps such as Smiling Mind or ReachOut Breathe can assist here.

Negative focus

She focuses on the negative, ignoring or misinterpreting the positive aspects of a situation – or, indeed, the facts. She sees only the weaknesses of those around her, and forgets or ignores their strengths. If her parents do anything positive, she filters out and rejects this and focuses exclusively on the downside.

> Charlotte is 18 and has been trying to lose weight. She was 'good' all last week, but yesterday she blew it and had a piece of cake for dessert. She feels like such a loser! She's convinced she can't do anything right. She has spent the day mulling over the fact that she shouldn't have eaten that piece of cake. She's decided to go off her diet and eat the rest of the cake, and all the chocolate in the pantry, then start the diet all over again tomorrow.

Negative thought patterns are repetitive, unproductive thoughts that serve no real purpose and directly cause negative emotions (emotions are a reflection of our thoughts, felt in the body). Parents can encourage their daughters to learn to recognise and identify these thought patterns as they occur and make choices about how to react. Teenagers can learn how to challenge the negative thought (for example, 'Nobody likes me') by saying, 'That's not a true statement. My family like me, and I have my friend from work and my friend from school. And I get on well with many other people now that I think of it. Also, not everybody will adore and admire me in this life. I accept that. It's the same for everybody. Besides, if somebody does think little of you, you don't have to agree with it . . .'

Jumping to conclusions

She interprets things negatively, even if there are no definite facts. She starts predicting the future and takes on the role of mind reader. She constantly predicts that bad things will happen.

> Toni is giving a speech in front of her class. A girl towards the back of the classroom yawns, so Toni goes home convinced that it was a terrible speech and that the entire audience was bored. She feels defeated, judged and swears she will never give another speech.

Parents can encourage their daughters to learn to recognise and identify this type of thought distortion and challenge it by looking at other possible explanations for the yawn (for example, she was tired), and that not everyone yawned and the feedback she got from the teacher was quite positive.

Rigid thinking

She tends to have fixed rules and unrealistic expectations, regularly using words like 'should', 'must' and 'can't'. This leads her to be constantly disappointed and angry with those in her orbit.

> Amber is kept waiting at school when her mother gets stuck in traffic. Her mum's mobile battery has run out, so she can't ring Amber to let her know she's running late. It starts to rain and with each passing second Amber becomes increasingly tense and angry. 'Why am I left standing here? Why didn't Mum ring? She's always late. She'd never do this to (sister) Lucy . . .' And when her mother finally arrives, she lets fly with a torrent of abuse.

Once again, Mum needs not to respond to the abuse; rather, when Amber has calmed down, state that sometimes traffic is heavy and she wasn't in a position to let her know. Acknowledge that this is upsetting and brainstorm with her what her alternatives in this situation might be.

As we saw in the first two chapters, part of the reason Princess B behaves in these ways is physiological – her body and brain are 'under construction', and she simply doesn't yet possess the mental tools to deal with everyday challenges in a constructive and non-confrontational manner. Yet we've also seen that there may be external factors at home, at school and in her online world that exacerbate and fuel Princess B's maladaptive behaviours. I want to turn now to some practical, evidence-based strategies for parenting your resident princess.

Part 2

Parenting
Princess B

Chapter 8

Styles of parenting

While many parents have honourable intentions, it seems that an increasing number of them raise teenage daughters via a curious mix of outsourcing, improvisation and hope. Of course, as mentioned earlier, almost all healthy teenage girls will test the boundaries once in a while – not least in order to figure out where the boundaries are and to see if they are still being enforced. This is also an opportunity for parents to determine whether current boundaries need to be adjusted.

But it seems that some otherwise rational parents indulge their daughters to the extent that they no longer register the demands being made on their time and energy. Worse, they don't seem to be able to see the challenging behaviours on display at home, at school and in public places, from doctor's waiting rooms to aeroplanes, bus stops and shopping centres. In my experience, many of these parents turn a blind eye because they simply do not know how to manage their own feelings, let alone the feelings of their children who would scream their protest if limits were placed on their behaviour. So these parents develop protective blinkers that block out all signs of their daughters' behavioural problems.

When children misbehaved in previous generations, a stern look from a parent would be enough to make most children stop. Today's parents can shoot a devastating look to their adolescent offspring, only to be met with a steely glare or, as likely as not, an exasperated eye-roll. We have arrived at a place where the fundamentals of parenting insofar as we understood them – to instil good manners and to ensure adequate sleep, good nutrition, exercise and fresh air – are no longer a given, because many parents hesitate to insist on them in case their offspring don't agree. Saying 'no' seems harsh to these parents. The tail is increasingly wagging the dog!

Why are so many parents afraid to set any kind of rules, limits or boundaries for their children? The answer lies partly in the promotion of parenting approaches such as permissive parenting, advocated by US paediatrician Dr Benjamin Spock in the 1950s and 1960s as a reaction against the authoritarian child-rearing practices of the past. Dr Spock's book *Baby and Child Care*, published in 1946, was one of the bestsellers of all time. Its message to parents was, 'You know more than you think you do'. The message of this book, however, is, 'Life is more compli-cated now and you need to know more'. The self-confessed insecurity of parents and their hunger for guidance indicate that these tactics simply have not worked. Many parents in the 21st century seem to be living in a vacuum of quiet desperation. The problems in schools, as hapless teachers try to discipline kids whose parents can't (or won't) try to limit them, and the pressures on doctors to prescribe drugs to regulate these children's objectionable behaviours are symptoms of the problem.

If we continue down the path of pharmaceutical straight jackets and 'Lindsay Lohan parenting', these girls will not learn conflict resolution, anger management or problem-solving strategies. They will not learn to take responsibility for their own behaviour (empathy is the key to moral development) or develop the internal resources to manage stress, loss, failure and disappointment (simple facts of life as we grow up). As a result, almost any bump in the road will knock them sideways.

WHAT'S YOUR SCRIPT?

Every parent has a 'parenting script' they learned when *they* were being brought up, which in turn often governs how they parent their own children. A parenting script has two main components: how *responsive* parents are, and how *demanding*. Being responsive means intentionally fostering a sense of individuality and self-management in your daughter: being attuned, supportive and attentive to her particular needs. The 'demanding' component (which is hugely problematic for many parents) refers to the boundaries and limits you set for your daughter: monitoring, providing adequate supervision, negotiating and consistently following through on a discipline system centred around accountability.

Social scientists have invented various names for the different parenting styles they have encountered, but the three parenting styles first identified by psychologist Diana Baumrind in the 1970s are still the most commonly used: permissive, authoritarian and authoritative, as well as uninvolved/neglectful (later added by Maccoby and Martin in 1983). Each of these parenting styles is not just the product of our own experience of being parented, but also of both parents' values and the practices and behaviours that flow from these. Of course, no parent uses one of these styles exclusively – we more often than not employ a mix of these approaches, depending on the age of our children, our family circumstances (sole-parent, blended, extended, etc.) and other factors. However, I include these here to encourage you to think about your overall approach and reflect on whether it may be contributing to the conflict you experience with your teenager.

Permissive

Permissive parents are more responsive than demanding. They are easygoing, lenient, often unconventional, do not practise or expect mature behaviour, and they make the (horrendous and erroneous) assumption that their daughter has the maturity to act in her long-term best interests. They avoid confrontation, and hide in their shell when conflict arises, shying away from anything that makes them feel negative emotions or discomfort. They labour under the misapprehension that they are doing the right thing, but in fact they are allowing situations to simmer and build up, ultimately making them more difficult to handle as time passes. A permissive parent can be conscientious, engaged and committed to his or her daughter, but often the main aim is to be her best friend.

And while it is true that all children need to feel a strong connection with their parents and to feel loved, they also need a regular dose of vitamin 'N' – in other words, they need to hear 'no'. If we try to be their 'mate', we will always put our need for them to like us before their need to learn to like themselves. So be a mentor, and help them learn what is safe and unsafe, and what is appropriate and inappropriate.

Authoritarian

Authoritarian parents are commanding and controlling, providing a well-ordered and structured environment with clearly stated rules. They tend to be very decisive, but are not responsive – they seek immediate compliance, and expect their orders to be obeyed without explanation. They demand conformity and reward quiet acceptance and dutifulness. Authoritarian parents expect their offspring to accept their judgements, values and goals without question. They are also more likely to use punishment to try to control their children's behaviour.

Most people (including our parents and grandparents) labour under the delusion that strict parenting/corporal punishment/reasonable chastisement magically produces better-behaved kids. However, research indicates that authoritarian parents raise children with low self-esteem who often behave more poorly than other kids, leading to even more punishment. Strict parenting actually creates behaviour problems in children. Setting draconian limits may momentarily control behaviour, but they don't help a child learn to self-regulate. Moreover, this type of authoritarian parenting is based on fear, with little or no empathy. If your teenager does what you want because they fear you, this is no different to bullying; if you yell, they will yell; if you use force, they will use force. They will learn to obey, but they won't learn to think for themselves. Authoritarian parenting makes it clear to children that a part of them is not acceptable, and that parents aren't available to help them learn to cope and manage difficult feelings. They're left lonely, isolated and trying to sort out for themselves how to overcome their 'lesser' impulses.

Adults raised in families where punitive discipline is used have been shown to exhibit tendencies towards anger and depression. They are more likely to be reluctant to question authority and are less likely to take responsibility for their actions.

Authoritative

Authoritative parents are both demanding and responsive. They impart and monitor clear standards for their children's conduct. They are firm, but not intrusive or restrictive: their disciplinary methods are supportive rather than punitive. They want their children to be assertive as well as socially responsible, and self-regulated as well as cooperative. Authoritative parents expect their children to behave appropriately, but are more open to give-and-take and to offer calm explanations of the rationale behind the limits and boundaries. Research indicates that authoritative parenting leads to positive developmental outcomes for adolescents.

An authoritative parent:

- says no when it is appropriate, even though saying yes would be much easier
- recognises that parents have rights
- is non-manipulative, i.e. sets limits, reasons with kids and is responsive to their emotional needs
- offers empathy rather than just sympathy
- encourages strengths rather than dwelling on weaknesses
- encourages free choice and the learning that comes from making mistakes
- uses consequential learning (which says, 'If you eat toast in bed, you must sleep with the crumbs')
- expects responsible behaviour.

Uninvolved/Neglectful

Uninvolved parents are generally neither responsive nor demanding. They believe that once their daughter can fend for herself, their job is to provide the necessities (food and shelter) but there is little or no emotional input. Uninvolved parenting may also be a consequence of parents dealing with their own issues, such as mental illness or substance abuse.

ARE YOU TRYING TO BE A BEST FRIEND?

Parents often tell me that they prefer not to be strict with their daughters because they had very strict upbringings themselves and hated their own parents. So they are far more lenient in the hope that their daughter won't feel the same way about them. But it's not a good idea to try to be a 'cool' mum or dad – it's your job to be a parent, not a friend. You may find it hard to believe, but your daughter is more likely to feel resentful towards you in the long term if you fail to set limits and simply let her have her way with everything. This is because she will not develop the resilience she needs to cope with life in the real world.

Almost everyone is acquainted with the 'helicopter' parents who swoop down to do their daughter's science project or are overly involved in her social life. But these notorious parents, forever floating over their children, are now morphing into so-called 'snowplough' parents, trying to remove all obstacles for their daughters even before they've started employment, university or TAFE. There are credible stories of parents being so dismayed over their daughter's mid-semester mark that they have called the academic staff to complain, followed by the department chair, followed by the academic dean. Boarding school staff often report that parents have called staff members to complain about trivial roommate disputes, not to mention complaints about excessive noise or lack of provision of gluten-free or other special foods. Employers report instances of parents accompanying their daughters to job interviews and asking to sit in.

A growing number of parents are reluctant to cut the psychological and emotional apron strings. Blame it on technology or anxiety or habit, but some parents remain so enmeshed that they deprive their teenagers of the opportunity to develop proficiency, a feeling of satisfaction and wellbeing. Instead they leave them anxious, depressed and ill-equipped to deal with matters both small and large. Recent research has shown that over-controlling parents undermine the competence and confidence of students and can negatively affect the teacher–student relationship. The result is a bevy of young women who have simply failed to develop the skills they need to become fully functioning adults.

I find it difficult to understand or relate to the 'I am my daughter's best friend' mothers' brigade, mainly because it is carved into the DNA of most teenage girls to, at some stage, test the rules. The appropriate response to this psychological stretching of wings is to uphold the rules, or at least engage calmly to renegotiate them if you believe it is necessary (see chapter 9). Once you stop setting boundaries with your daughter, it will be impossible to rein her back in. How confusing is it for her if you fluctuate between best friend and parent? Leave her friends to be her friends – you need to be her parent.

Yet, being a parent doesn't mean being distant and cold. It is absolutely crucial to be accessible, open and non-judgemental as a parent – this inspires your daughter to engage with you. Your role is to uphold your daughter's individual value and worth, and to meet her emotional needs. But this type of support must always be one-way. Parents should never use their teenage daughter as a sounding board or resident counsellor. Daughters should not feel responsible for their mother's psychological health, for example, or burdened with parental problems.

Parents who routinely dump personal problems on their adolescent daughters are being too dependent on them for their own emotional needs. Find your own friends. I have never met a 15-year-old girl who really wants a 50-year-old friend. Mothers who are desperate to be their daughter's BFF are creating a generation of dependent and indulged young women ill-equipped to cope with the adult world. Don't be a parent who is so terrified of rocking the domestic boat that the word 'no' doesn't enter your vocabulary.

> My husband and I both have demanding jobs and we feel a bit guilty about often being home late and not having much 'family life' with our 14-year-old daughter, Mia. On the one hand, we figure she's doing better than a lot of other kids because she's pretty free to do what she likes, she gets plenty of pocket money and we often buy her a surprise to make up for not being around. But a close friend of mine recently suggested that Mia is becoming spoilt. When I asked her to explain what she meant, my friend told me that Mia had been very cruel to one of the friends in her group, intentionally leaving her out of social events and generally behaving in a critical and spiteful way. I was quite shocked by this, as she is a high-achieving, pretty and charming girl and doesn't need to behave this way.

A lot of parents make this mistake – that is, they try to win or buy their daughter's affection and approval. This often seems to stem, at least in part, from a sense of guilt at not choosing to spend enough time with her. If you feel this might be happening in your household, redefine what taking care of your daughter means, and what it looks like. Consider her emotional and spiritual needs rather than her 'need' for material things, and work at making yourself emotionally available. For example, if she tells you about her day, stop what you are doing and listen. Be physically and emotionally present for her. Maintain a sense of routine and normality in the home – this offers the safe haven that adolescents need from the multiple whirlwinds they navigate on a daily basis.

ARE YOU HOVERING?

Despite the relative rarity of violent crimes against a person, many girls live highly orchestrated lives. They are driven to school, for example, instead of walking or taking public transport, as well as being driven to and from every social event, day and night. Plus, their mobile phones (paid for by parents) become like the world's longest umbilical cords, attaching girls to their anxious mothers who text them frequently to see 'how they are going'. This is the so-called 'bubble-wrap generation'.

Yet, as we have seen, raising children to be resilient adults means giving them opportunities to manage risk, to endure accidents, and to overcome setbacks. This cannot occur if they are raised in a bubble. How do kids learn to ride a bike? By falling off! How do kids learn to deal with pain? By being hurt. How do kids learn to assess risk? By being exposed to danger. How do kids develop immunity? By being exposed to germs.

At some level this must make sense to parents, yet many are hamstrung by their own fear of pain, risk and danger and simply cannot tolerate the idea of their children experiencing these. They deem it their primary function to level the track, removing all of the hurdles so that their child will never have to withstand any adversities, hardships and other difficulties along their path in life.

None of this is conscious, of course. These parents have never wondered why they have such a powerful urge to protect their children. To such a question they might respond, 'It's just natural, isn't it?' As a psychologist, part of my job is helping parents understand how their unconscious drives and motivations play out in their relationships with their children. Such a determination to try and control a teenage girl almost always ends in tears, as these attempts inevitably trigger defensiveness that not only shuts down communication, but simply results in an increased attempt to break away and defy boundaries. It's really emancipation on steroids – the teenager just ends up pushing harder to separate from her family, the emotional temperature rises through the roof and anger becomes the language of the relationship.

> I'm twelve and my parents won't let me do anything!
> I can't have a conversation without Mum interrupting;
> I can't go for walks with my friends or be left alone at
> home for too long. All we do is sit around inside, and
> all they do is worry about what will happen to me if I
> so much as step outside the front door. Mum drives

me everywhere, even to the local shopping centre,
which is, like, 50 metres away! I think it's because I am
a girl and I am small for my age, so they think people
will pick on me. It's annoying and embarrassing.

Independence from parents is critical for a teenager's
psychological and social development. Young girls need
time and space to explore, climb trees and solve problems
in real-life situations. If we fail to offer developmentally
appropriate opportunities to do so, we are effectively
telling them that we don't have confidence in their own
ability to look after themselves – the result of which is
that they will feel helpless, rather than cared for. As a
consequence, teenagers are increasingly escaping via
cyberspace, which is largely unsupervised; while they may
not be allowed to walk to the local supermarket, thanks
to the internet they can communicate with anyone and
everyone in the 'safety' of their own home. A more rational approach seems to be in order.

IS IT TOO LATE TO CHANGE YOUR STYLE?

When children are younger, they necessarily depend
on you for everything, and are happy enough to let you
make all the decisions. The arrival of the teenage years,
of course, necessitates a very different approach. Some
parents, however, don't seem to realise that a shift in
parenting style is required until something untoward
happens. In the case of Princess B, her primary goal is to
achieve independence. To do this, she needs to separate
especially from the parent she was closest to. Parents

without this developmental perspective often feel on a constant war footing or personalise the fact that Princess B would rather be anywhere but around them (like she used to). As she matures, she will start to form her own moral code, and her parents may become upset when she develops her own strong opinions and starts to assert herself – all in the name of fighting against parental control. Parents faced with this maturational mutiny may need to examine how much room they give Princess B to be an individual. Clinicians often try to get parents to ask questions such as, 'Am I too controlling?', 'Do I listen to my child?' and 'Do I allow my teenager's opinions and tastes to differ from my own?'

Parenting a teenager is much easier if you think of yourself as a guide rather than a dictator. Your role is to provide boundaries that you negotiate together but that you are still prepared to enforce. As we saw in Part 1, it also helps if you maintain a developmental perspective. This means:

- understanding that your daughter's brain is a work in progress, and that the risk-taking behaviour and impulsivity she exhibits as a result of this can cause mood swings and fuel conflict and anger
- recognising that she is on a voyage of self-discovery, which involves novelty-seeking behaviour, and that it's normal for her to want to take a chainsaw to the apron strings
- respecting her opinions even when you don't agree with them

- thinking back to how you felt and behaved as a teenager and admitting to yourself any hypocrisy
- tolerating the mildly irritating behaviours (clothes left in the bathroom, losing things, plates festering under the bed) that are common to young people; tidiness needs a sophisticated level of cognitive control, and the way your daughter's teenage brain is connected means that her planning is not very good.

Most adolescents will try out new ideas that may be unacceptable to their parents – this is a normal part of identity formation rather than a deliberate attempt to annoy you. Even when you have a warm relationship with your daughter, some conflict inevitably occurs, much of it the low-level griping around their desire for increased independence and autonomy. Like a toddler, she has become very aware of her new abilities and widening range of choices. She says 'no' simply because she can.

In the next chapter, I want to look at the parenting strategies you can adopt to help you move closer to an authoritative parenting style.

Chapter 9
Strategies that work

In my clinical practice I have worked with countless parents frustrated by their adolescent daughter's behaviour, and I have come to understand that the issue is more often about helping parents change their own parenting script, rather than attempting to change their daughter's behaviour. Often, when I first start working with parents I give them this 'parent power quiz', asking them to tick yes or no for each question.

I can prevent my daughter from going out.	Yes	No
I can choose her friends.	Yes	No
I can make sure she studies hard.	Yes	No
I can prevent her from smoking and drinking.	Yes	No
I can stop her from listening to loud music.	Yes	No
I can prevent her from using illicit drugs.	Yes	No
I can prevent her from having sex.	Yes	No
I can prevent her from getting pregnant.	Yes	No
I can stop her from drink-driving.	Yes	No
I can make her go to university.	Yes	No

If they answer 'yes' to any of these questions, I very gently break it to them that they are living in la-la land. Parents have no genuine power over what their teenage daughters like or feel, where they go or what they do outside of the home. This fact does not, however, stop parents from continuing to attempt to gain the upper hand by using an assortment of weapons including guilt trips, grounding, humiliation, shouting, threats and character assassination. Yet the truth is that such techniques (if they work at all) achieve nothing more than short-term, superficial and limited control. At the same time, they run the risk of reaping aggression, rebellion and/or estrangement and impacting on a child's self-esteem. Instead, armed with a developmental perspective and with accurate, up-to-date and reliable information, parents can feel much more confident about staying in control of their own feelings and offering stability and support.

Strategically changing your parenting script, letting go of control over things that don't matter, allowing your daughter privacy and space, and letting her learn from her mistakes will all help to avoid the Princess Bitchface Syndrome. A parent who takes a developmental perspective understands this, and avoids turning everything into a huge issue. This ultimately ensures a better quality of life for the whole family.

It will take time to relearn the parenting script you inherited and to confidently implement these new strategies. Many of them may appear obvious, but under stress good sense can be forgotten. Parents are allowed to make mistakes – there is no such thing as a perfect parent.

The trick is to learn from these mistakes and not make the same ones over and over again. Give yourself time, and do remember that most young people are very forgiving.

1. ENCOURAGE RESILIENCE

Resilience is the ability to bounce back and try again after a setback, to pick yourself up, dust yourself off and keep going, no matter how hard you fell. It's also about being willing to have a go at something new, and to be open to asking someone for help. It's not about being brave or strong, but simply feeling okay about yourself – knowing that you will be okay with whatever life dishes up. In other words, it is our ability to adapt to stress, and the less stressed we are, the happier we are.

Young children learn resilience through their family relationships: by feeling supported and loved; by watching their parents talk to each other, listen to each other, express feelings and resolve conflict; by being encouraged to think positively; and by being given opportunities to make mistakes, miss out and cope with disappointment.

By the time your daughter reaches early adolescence, you will have a fair idea of how well she copes with adversity. If she demonstrates any of the following in her upper primary years, her chances of struggling at secondary school are much greater:

- She does not cope well with school (academically or socially) in year 5 or year 6.
- She does not feel safe, valued or listened to at home.

- She has trouble obtaining, maintaining and retaining friendships.
- She has learning difficulties.
- She does not participate in activities such as art, music, dance, drama or sport.

Apart from providing ongoing support and love, there are a couple of other things you can do to help your daughter develop a stronger, more resilient sense of self. These are outlined below.

Help her find her spark

Adolescence is a key time for a girl to find her 'spark', described by Dr Peter Benson as something that the child is naturally good at, comes easily to them and that they love doing. If supported, this activity provides the child with incredible joy, motivation and direction.

There are three types of spark:

- a natural skill or talent, such as playing a musical instrument or sport, performing dance or drama, or creating artwork
- a commitment, such as volunteering or being environmentally conscious
- an aspect of character, such as being empathetic or a good listener.

These 'islands of competence' (a term first coined by Harvard psychologist Dr Robert Brooks) not only allow girls to take healthy risks and socialise with friends who are a positive influence, but also greatly increase the likelihood of them forming a healthy relationship with another charismatic adult, such as a teacher or coach. It also provides an alternative outlet and friendship group, which can be helpful for girls dealing with cliques (see page 42). Having something that she loves to do that gives her a sense of purpose will help free your daughter from the need for approval that haunts many girls and diminishes their confidence.

The problem is that many parents, when their daughters reach this age, spend less time with them – when in fact their active involvement is desirable because it is a key period in helping girls find what makes them truly happy.

Finding her spark also enables her to experience 'flow' – that wonderful state where she is so immersed in what she is doing that she does not notice the passing of time. Also known as 'the zone', flow is the mental state of operation in which a person performing an activity is fully immersed in a feeling of energised focus, full involvement and enjoyment in the process of the activity. In essence, when your daughter is in 'flow', she is completely absorbed and loving what she's doing.

In her excellent book *Girls Uninterrupted*, Tanith Carey suggests that if you are not sure what your early adolescent's spark is, there's a simple way to know – ask her what she loves to do. If she is too young to work it out for herself, watch what activities totally absorb her. Then support and encourage her to engage in these activities at every opportunity.

Widen the circle of care

As a way of mitigating the psychological pain of independence, a great strategy is to widen the network of caring adults around your daughter by including and involving specific women friends and relatives in your daughter's life. The idea is that in doing so, your daughter will feel encouraged to share problems and confide in other 'charismatic adults'. The literature has many references to the importance in girls' lives of their 'best friend's mum' and this is a logical extension of that idea. Girls do not always get on well with their mothers and do not feel they can discuss certain subjects with them. Steve Biddulph, in his book *Raising Girls*, talks about these women as the 'aunties army' – a wonderful concept.

2. NEGOTIATE THE RULES

As we have seen, our daughters' transitions from girlhood to adolescence can be a very trying time. The innocent questions of childhood give way to feisty opinions – *lots* of opinions. As parents we feel that we are not needed anymore – she insists that she has all the answers and no longer needs our guidance. Yet Princess B's antics make it clear that we still need to set limits on behaviour because her voice of reason has yet to develop. Put simply, parents have the right to point out that there are lines that aren't to be crossed and that there are consequences if they are crossed. All parents have the right (and obligation) to try to keep their daughters safe.

As long as she is living under your roof, make it clear that she must be accountable for her actions, and that you do have a right to monitor what she does and where she goes. However much you trust her, it's a special type of crazy to let her loose in the world without any boundaries. At the same time, when negotiating what she's allowed to do and where she's allowed to go, you initially need to believe that she will behave well. Tell her that you trust her to behave appropriately at all times, and that you expect her to respect this.

Rules are needed in every family so that each member knows what contributions they need to make to keep their home a safe and comfortable place to live. Girls should know exactly what is expected of them, such as when homework should be done, when bed sheets should be changed and laundry put out, what time they should be home, whether they should be earning their own spending money and how. However, the days of parents 'laying down the law' are long gone, and it is now accepted that it is more effective for parents and adolescents to negotiate boundaries and sanctions *together*. So, as early as possible, you must sit down with your teenager and draw up any rules that relate to her safety and health (e.g. sex, alcohol, diet, drugs, exercise, curfews, sleep, internet use and study). In this way, she will feel that she has some ownership of the arrangements and is more likely to stick to them. State clearly what the boundaries are, but be prepared to negotiate and review them from time to time. Ideally there is a gradual loosening of the reins, where you reward her good behaviour and demonstrated responsibility with greater freedom. You might, for instance, insist that a

14-year-old be home by 9 p.m., but extend the curfew each year thereafter.

Base the rules on family values

Family values will inevitably influence the house rules. For instance, in some families it will be important for the whole family to attend religious services together, whereas in others it might be optional. Some families might have more laid-back rules about pocket money, parties or housework than others. It's important that parents review their values to see if they really are values or just traditions. If they are values, teenage girls will benefit from having rules that reflect them.

Avoid excessive or unrealistic rules

There is no point in having rules that you have no ability to enforce, such as rules about who your daughter may hang out with at school. Also, be wary of having too many rules. Sometimes parents have so many rules that they couldn't possibly have time to monitor, let alone enforce them, which almost always guarantees that your daughter will be able to get around them. It's better to have fewer rules that are consistently enforced than many rules that are haphazardly enforced, if at all.

Be prepared to update the rules

If your daughter is complaining about a rule, invite her to talk about how she would like to see the rule changed. It is crucial that the onus is on her to convince you: if she offers a thoughtful argument in favour of changing her curfew from 10 p.m. to midnight, say so and agree. If she fails to convince you, you can tell her so, but suggest that she feel free to come back later with another argument. At least she will feel listened to and less inclined to enter into the characteristic power struggle over this issue.

3. USE PRE-AGREED CONSEQUENCES

Consequences should be agreed beforehand, and should be fair and reasonable, as too severe an outcome will invite her to rebel. In other words, don't go overboard – if she breaks a curfew, for example, she might have to stay in the next night, but not for the next month. If consequences are too excessive, they will be seen as punishments, which doesn't teach your daughter anything except to avoid the punisher (and no doubt, to develop revenge fantasies). The system should be used to change behaviour, not to make you feel better by getting revenge.

Make the consequences as natural or logical as possible; for example, if she runs out of credit on her prepaid mobile phone, she'll soon find herself unable to text her friends. This is where you can also get creative. If she continually leaves her belongings all over the house, they may be picked up and placed in the freezer and/or a 'butler charge' may be deducted from her allowance.

Grounding your daughter for a month, or banning the internet for two weeks might seem like good ideas at the time but are virtually impossible to police. When consequences are difficult to enforce, you run the risk of not following through or following through inconsistently. Even worse, you may throw in the towel altogether – which means you lose your credibility and your daughter will feel that you cannot be trusted.

Some parents seek to rescue their daughters from even the most benign consequences, worrying that it will somehow scar them for life if they have to walk home because they spent their train fare on junk food, or can't text friends for two weeks because they blew all their phone credit. The truth is quite the opposite – by interfering with the laws of cause and effect, parents are actually denying their children opportunities for growth.

> My daughter Nirvana and I were always close, so much
> so that my friends used to joke that we were joined at
> the hip. Then when she got to secondary school every-
> thing seemed to change. She'd bring her school laptop
> home and spend all her time talking to her friends
> on social media. She wouldn't do anything around
> the house – even load the dishwasher or walk the
> dog – and would be rude whenever we asked. I tried to
> be strict with her (her father is a business executive and
> is hardly ever at home). I made a list of chores and put
> it on the fridge door, but I always end up doing every-
> thing myself. Her father and I argue about how to best
> deal with the situation. I keep hoping it is hormonal,
> just a phase, but she is becoming increasingly out of
> control. I'm just about at the end of my tether.

However well intentioned, Nirvana's parents are contributing to her behaviour. First up, her mother should

stop doing the chores assigned to Nirvana. Parents should refrain as much as possible from doing things for their daughter if she is capable of doing them herself. Both parents need to think about what it is that Nirvana values, and recognise that a (psychological) carrot is always going to be better than a stick. A good strategy is for parents to take the things their children value and make these conditional upon things that they don't value, like doing chores. In Nirvana's case it's using social media, so I suggest that the laptop be made unavailable for a time. Nirvana has to learn that when she chooses bad behaviour, she also chooses the consequences.

4. SAY 'NO' AND MEAN IT

Nowhere is it written that parents must provide their daughters with a new smartphone every year, buy her whatever clothing/makeup/jewellery her friends have, or drive her and her friends anywhere (commonly referred to as 'uber parenting'). Our primary job is to prepare our daughters for the real world. Not everyone has pearly white teeth, you don't always get what you want and emotional problems can't be solved by spending money. Your daughter does not have to love you every minute of the day – we all get over the disappointment of being told 'No', but she won't find it so easy to get over the effects of being indulged. Waiting for what you want (or delayed gratification) is part of adult life and she will be better equipped to deal with it later if she's been introduced to the notion while growing up.

Be consistent

Once you say no, you need to stick to your decision. As we saw in chapter 8, Princess B has some corrosive strategies that she may employ to wear you down until, for the sake of peace, you give in. When parenting, if you say you will do something and you do it, or you won't do something and you don't do it, you will win your daughter's trust. In the same way, the opposite is true, and she will learn that you are not to be trusted. As a result, you will lose credibility and she will start to ignore everything you say. We teach people how to treat us. If she sees you as consistent, trustworthy and credible, she will also believe that you are willing to follow through with consequences, even if she has never actually seen you do so.

Don't be a doormat

Parents need to have a notion of themselves as separate human beings worthy of respect. This is necessary not only for our own mental health, but also to be good role models for our children. If you tolerate abuse from your adolescent, you teach them that it is okay to treat people this way.

If your daughter expresses her lust for independence via a lack of respect and consideration for others, inside or outside of the family, this should not be ignored. Disrespect is not a sign of independence but of immaturity (she is, after all, still learning the delicate balancing act of diplomacy, as well as the ability to rein in strong emotion). Accepting, let alone making excuses for her bad behaviour, will in no way help her to find her psychological footing: you should respond in the same way you would to any adult who spoke to you rudely or treated you badly. If she does not learn limits from her parents, she is sure to learn them later, and much more harshly, from others in society.

While this may sometimes sound like a tall order, the last thing a girl needs is parents who are afraid of her or who act as unpaid servants. The tail must never be allowed to wag the dog. Even though they may appear to be working very hard to undermine your authority, adolescents can actually become confused and frightened if they succeed. This is because they don't yet have the skills, knowledge or experience to handle the power they feel they have. When parents show that they don't know what to do, that they have no power or that they are scared, their daughter's natural response is to become stressed and frightened, too. For many of the young women I see in my practice, this results in an escalation of their acting-out behaviours in order to force their parents to resume their parenting role.

> Fourteen-year-old Georgie attended the local state
> school, and her early years as the middle child of
> three had been uneventful. Her mum and dad were
> both teachers. They were astonished when she started
> truanting and hanging out with a group of older
> disaffected and disaffiliated teens who introduced her
> to sex, drugs, street art and the 'exciting' nightlife of
> homeless young people in her town. She began staying
> away for days at a time and stealing money from her
> siblings and parents. When they sought to restrict

her nocturnal activities she made multiple threats of self-harm, including threats to take her own life. She refused all offers of help from medical or psychological professionals. Terrified, they sought to appease her, giving her a phone, money and food. She responded by making completely unfounded accusations of abuse and, despite all attempts by police, social services and youth workers, she became increasingly estranged from the family and contact became more and more sporadic. Her parents ended up exhausted and the toll on the family mounted to the point that her father suffered a myocardial infarction and went on extended leave. The situation deteriorated and all contact with Georgie was lost. The family reluctantly gave up on trying to have a reconciliation and, at the time of writing, the family have not heard from her, although there have been unconfirmed sightings of her in another city.

5. COMMUNICATE WITH RESPECT

It's important, from the moment she is able to string two words together, to talk to your daughter about everyday issues such as school, sport, music and hobbies. If you don't encourage conversation with her about these things, it will be harder for her to discuss the things that worry her later.

This is a two-way street. If she remembers you as always being prepared to listen (in a non-judgemental manner) without making things seem trivial or an over-reaction, there is a much greater chance of keeping the communication lines open. Moreover, the only way your daughter will respect your views is if you value hers. By discussing sex and drug issues at home, you will have more opportunities to offer guidance on the subject. (To give good guidance on sensitive issues, try to be as informed as possible: see the Resources section at the end of this book.)

Listen attentively

If you are fortunate enough to be parenting a teenage girl who is still willing to share what is happening in her life, make sure you listen attentively. This means taking the time to stop what you are doing and giving her your full attention. Even if you disagree with what she is saying, listening without interrupting gets the conversation off to a positive start.

So how do we listen attentively?

1. Stand or sit close to them.
2. Make eye contact.
3. Clear your mind and concentrate on what your daughter is saying, rather than on what you want to say.
4. Let your child finish speaking without interruption.
5. Show her you are interested, even if you think you know where the conversation is headed, by nodding, smiling or saying things like, 'I see' or 'Really?' or 'Oh!'
6. Wait until your child has finished before asking a question.

When we listen attentively to our children, they feel valued and worthwhile. It also strengthens our connection with them, so that they feel secure. A child who feels a positive, strong connection to her parents is less likely to act out against their attempts to set limits.

Acknowledge her feelings

It is an understatement to say that many teenage girls experience volatile moods. These extremes of emotion usually settle over time, but until they do you should avoid asking questions such as, 'What is the matter with you?' and 'What's suddenly gotten into you?' Not only are these unanswerable, but they also aggravate the situation. Even if she does know what the problem is, she's hardly likely to say: 'Look, I am torn by conflicting emotions, affected by structural changes in my brain, engulfed by irrational urges and confused by raging hormones.'

When your daughter is communicating feelings of anger, disappointment, fear or grief, a powerful strategy is to use reflective listening. This means acknowledging her emotions without trying to fix them, without trying to force her to feel differently and without distracting her from how she is feeling. Listen to what she is saying and try to understand what is happening for her, and then respond without judgement. For example:

- 'I can see that you are really upset about this.'
- 'Oh, that must be hard.'
- 'I can see that you are very sad about this.'
- 'You seem angry about what happened.'

This may look easy on the page, but can be a real challenge, especially if you are the kind of person who is uncomfortable with strong, negative emotions – yours or anyone else's. Many parents may withdraw, rescue, distract or even reprimand their daughters in an effort to avoid those feelings, which only reinforces the idea that these emotions are 'bad'.

But as all psychologists know, negative emotions are an important adaptive response – they help us to evaluate our experiences – and the harder we push them away, the stronger they become. The key is to accept that they are there, which frees us to find more adaptive solutions to our problems. However, we still need to set limits on the behavioural expression of emotion. Your daughter needs to know that it's okay to be angry, but it's not okay to be violent or nasty or cruel – physical and verbal abuse and the destruction of property are definitely out.

Stay calm

As hard as it might be, try to remember that when your daughter is giving you a look of sheer hatred or has just unleashed a torrent of unflattering metaphors about your performance as a parent, it's more that she is upset, confused and angry at your attempts to set limits. It is her job to test boundaries and you need to remember that she is still on training wheels when it comes to regulating her emotions. This doesn't mean you condone abusive behaviour – she needs to learn that it is not okay to speak to people in this way – but she is not going to learn this if *you* fly off the handle and can't show her how to regulate emotions.

How you express yourself and what you say to your daughter, especially when you are angry, will inhibit or improve your relationship with her. It is important to respond in a way that models respectful communication and concentrates on the behaviour, not the person. Resist the urge to use put-downs or sarcasm – no matter how many she directs at you. All adolescents have an inbuilt sensitivity to being belittled, and parents who repeatedly push this button will raise the heat until they've created an emotional bonfire.

Lower your voice rather than raise it, maintain eye contact and adopt a non-threatening physical posture. If you feel yourself losing control, withdraw from the situation with a disengagement line, such as: 'We're both getting upset now. Let's stop and talk again later.'

If you find yourself constantly triggered by your daughter's anger, it might be helpful to look at some strategies for managing your own.

Anger management 101

Many of us have been brought up to believe that displays of emotion are a sign of weakness and must be avoided at all costs. So when a child is crying or screaming, we start yelling at them to stop and the whole situation escalates until someone lashes out physically (a slammed door, a slap or worse). In these situations, you need some strategies to manage your own anger before you can even begin to help them manage theirs.

Of course, we all get angry at our children, sometimes furious. But we are the adults in the situation – our job is to control the expression of our anger and therefore minimise its negative impact. This isn't always easy, especially when we're flooded with fight-or-flight hormones and our muscles are tense, our pulse is racing, our breath quickened and we're ready to either clobber someone or run a marathon. No matter how hard it is to stay calm at these moments, we know that the last thing we want to do is hurt our kids. We need to walk away, take time out, remove ourselves from the situation so that we don't hit, swear, use name-calling or sarcasm or scream at our kids. When your kids watch you deal constructively with your anger, they'll learn how to handle their own rage. You'll become a role model for your child, showing them that anger is part of being human, and that learning to manage anger responsibly is part of becoming a *mature* human being.

Unfortunately, some people never manage to master their anger, and they carry this infantile rage with them through a thousand road rage incidents and ugly, spiteful confrontations with telephone operators, shop assistants and work colleagues. Sadly, this ends up impacting their children, who adopt the same template for problem-solving – and so the cycle continues.

Watch for warning signs

Many parents tell me they explode into anger without warning, but there are almost always warning signs in the body. Paying attention to the way anger feels in your body helps you to recognise when your temper is starting to boil and allows you to take steps to manage your anger before it gets out of control. You might feel a knot in your stomach, clench your jaw, feel hot and sweaty, or get a headache. Some people can pace around the house, while others literally see red, have trouble concentrating, or their heart may pound or their shoulders become tense. Parents, in my experience, tend to lose it more easily when they are tired or their immune systems are compromised.

Notice thought triggers

Sometimes it might seem that situations cause us to feel angry (especially when other people are intentionally cruel, or things go wrong), but anger has less to do with what happens to us and more to do with how we *interpret* what happens – in other words, how we think about a situation. Common thinking patterns that trigger and fuel anger include the following.

Over-generalising

You view a challenging situation as an all-pervasive disaster that exists for all time, not just a problem at one particular moment. For example:

> *You ALWAYS interrupt me.*
> *You NEVER consider my needs.*
> *EVERYONE disrespects me.*
> *I NEVER get the credit I deserve.*

Rigid thinking

Whenever you use the words 'should' or 'must' it's a clue that you are more likely to get angry when reality doesn't line up with your vision. For example:

> *But it's not supposed to be done that way.*
> *You must do what I'm asking.*
> *I should be there already.*

Jumping to conclusions

You assume you know what someone else is thinking or feeling, and assume that he or she has intentionally upset you, ignored your wishes or disrespected you.

Collecting negatives

You collect things to get upset about, usually while overlooking anything positive, and letting these small irritations build and build until you explode, often over something relatively minor.

Righteous indignation

You tend to blame others when something bad happens or something goes wrong, rather than taking responsibility for your own behaviour.

Call time out

When you feel close to losing it, stop, take a deep breath and, in an even tone, say:

> *I'm too angry to talk about this now. I'm going*
> *to calm down and then we can talk.*
> *I can see you are upset. Let's stop now and talk*
> *about it later.*

Then move to another part of the house, or another place if you are outside your home. Some parents worry that walking away from an argument may appear to be a sign of low emotional intelligence – that they are afraid of strong emotions and need to exit. This is not the case at all. By naming the emotion ('I am feeling too angry') and choosing to walk away, you will impress upon your child just how serious the situation is, and you will also model self-control.

When you are away from your child, use this time to *calm down*, not to work yourself into a self-righteous frenzy about how wronged you feel. Get a glass of water, cuddle the dog – whatever dials it down.

Challenge your self-talk

Now tell yourself to get a grip: this is not an emergency – kids need our love most when they seem to deserve it least, and they desperately need our help to learn to manage emotions. Recognising that your current way of thinking might be self-defeating (i.e. it doesn't make you feel good or help you to get what you want) can sometimes motivate you to look at things from a different perspective. Here are the four main types of challenging questions to ask yourself:

1. Test the reality:
   Can I know for certain that what I'm thinking is true? Am I jumping to negative conclusions?
2. Look for alternative explanations:
   Are there any other ways that I could look at this situation?

If I were being positive, how would I perceive this situation?

3. Put things in perspective:
   Is there anything good about this situation?
   Will this matter in five years' time?
4. Use goal-directed thinking:
   Is this way of thinking helping me to achieve my goals?
   Is there something I can do to improve this situation?

Speak calmly

When you have calmed down, go back to your teenager and discuss what happened. If you've decided that the situation is worth getting angry about and there's something you can do to avoid or improve things, the key is to express your feelings in a healthy way. When communicated respectfully and channelled effectively, anger can be a tremendous source of energy and inspiration for change. Research shows that the more calmly we speak, the calmer we feel and the more calmly others respond to us. Using profanities and sarcasm might feel satisfying at the time (and we may think this is fine because at least we're not hitting our kids, right?), but this character assassination not only escalates emotions, but also damages the connection we have with our teenagers.

In every interaction with our children, we have the power to calm or exacerbate the situation by what we say and how we say it. Our kids may be spectacularly irritating, but we are not helpless victims. As parents we must learn to manage our own feelings first. Your daughter may not become a little angel overnight, but her acting out will diminish dramatically once you learn to stay calm.

If, after all your efforts, you still feel angry, look for the underlying feelings. Every time a child pushes your buttons, you can be sure those buttons were installed some time in your own childhood. Anger is always a defence, shielding us from feeling hurt or afraid and protecting us from feeling vulnerable. Once you get to the underlying feelings, your anger will dissipate. This is where professional help might be a good idea. Seek help if:

- you feel constantly frustrated and angry no matter what you try
- your temper causes problems in your relationships at home or at work
- your anger has led to police or legal troubles
- your anger has ever led to physical violence.

My daughter and I always seem to be fighting these days. She's sometimes so pigheaded and rude that I can't help getting angry and yelling, which I know is not good behaviour for a father. Nine times out of ten she loses it too and just yells back. It's like a vicious circle.

It's not at all unusual for teenage girls to fight with their fathers. But to say, as in the above scenario, that fathers can't help themselves isn't true: it's a matter of choice. Fathers can choose to respond by yelling, in which case she will do the same. If, as a parent, you really want to change the pattern that has developed, use your fully wired adult brain cells and make a different choice – walk away. Rather than responding in a negative way, simply say, in a clear and non-aggressive voice, 'I don't want to argue with you. I'll come back when things have calmed down.' Try it!

TOP TIPS FOR MINIMISING CONFLICT WITH TEENS

The best strategy for minimising conflict with teens is to have a strong connection with them. This doesn't mean that you control their every move or that they display a fearful, cloying dependence. It simply means that you are able to talk to one another so that you can find a workable solution to whatever led to the conflict in the first place. Other strategies to minimise conflict are as follows.

1. Choose a neutral location

If you need to engage in a robust discussion, choose a location other than the family home. This helps to avoid what psychologists call 'situational cues', or signals that a person should behave or respond in a particular way or that an action will occur. For example, if you stand in the doorway of your teenager's bedroom and sigh loudly, this may be a cue to your daughter that she is about to get the 'bedroom lecture'. Instead, go to a cafe or for a walk in the park. Find an excuse to go for a drive – the combination of a lack of eye contact, rolling scenery and no escape route can be the ideal scenario for engaging your teenager in a conversation.

2. Choose your battles

Don't argue over trivial things. No one has ever died from having an untidy room or wearing the same pair of underpants two days in a row, so be sure to choose your battles on the basis of whether the issue will impact on your child's health and safety.

3. De-escalate the situation

Great solutions to problems don't arise when we're feeling furious and frustrated, but when each party has cooled down and is ready to negotiate. Our IQ actually drops when we are angry, so we're working with a lot fewer tools in the toolbox. Your teenager relies on you to take the lead, so here's what to do:

1. State your feelings:
   I'm getting upset; let's leave it and talk later.
2. Listen attentively and get the facts:
   I see what you mean . . .
3. Acknowledge your teen's feelings, experience and point of view:
   Let me see if I've understood. I think you're saying you feel . . .
4. Be supportive:
   Don't forget I'm on your side . . .
5. Make it clear it's not about winning:
   Let's finish the argument now, but I want you to have the last word.

4. Be a mentor, not a mate

Adults who are uncomfortable with the strong emotions of adolescence often go for sarcasm and teasing, which are the purview of their peers (a.k.a. immature) and will usually shut down the very communication you are trying to keep open. If you like to use humour, make sure that it is upbeat and that you are actually funny! So be yourself, while maintaining a professional manner – adolescents expect adults to be an authority, but not authoritarian.

5. Avoid ultimatums

While it may be tempting to use the 'put-your-foot-down, no-negotiation' technique, or to deliver ultimatums – 'Do this or else!' – teenagers are especially sensitive to control, and will almost always reject an authoritarian approach.

6. Address the problem, not the person

Don't accuse, insult or talk down to your teenager, and be conscious of your tone of voice, facial expression, demeanour and body language.

When tempers flare, old resentments are often dragged onto the bonfire. Use reflective listening to keep your teenager focused on the problem at hand, and the need for you to work together to find a solution.

7. Be on the same page as your partner

The best approach, especially with a teenager, is to always give the impression that everyone involved in the conflict is on the same page, whether the parties are in complete disagreement or not. Save your parenting debates for pillow talk! A common disagreement for parents is at what age their teenage daughter can have a romantic interest sleep over. Dads often have the view that this will never happen while they have breath in their body, while mothers may have a more liberal view. The child needs to believe everyone is in agreement because if they can find the smallest loophole in any situation, they will by nature exploit it. United you stand. Divided, you are cactus.

Chapter 10

Common issues

In this chapter I want to look at some of the routine situations in the home that often result in low-level conflict and what to do about them. Conflict with your teenager can arise over anything. Key areas include all of the things most of interest to adolescents. In order of sensitivity, these are: peers, school, family and the internet (social media). It is worth doing a psychological inventory and asking yourself which areas can go through to the proverbial wicketkeeper. Wisely choosing battlegrounds and getting consensus from partners can mean that parenting doesn't have to be an exercise in martyrdom. If you give up trying to control things and avoid engaging in conflict, your daughter will come to realise that being cooperative isn't a threat to her independence.

THE BEDROOM BATTLE

'Clean up your room' is the classic opening shot for a parent–child standoff. However, teenagers desperately need their own space. It's time to accept that your child has the right to use her room in her own way. If she never tidies her bedroom, preferring a 'floordrobe', there'll come a point where she feels so frustrated at not being able to find things (or simply needs some space to entertain her friends) that she'll have a massive clean-up.

What to do

- Lead by example – if you keep things organised and tidy elsewhere in the house, chances are she will eventually do the same. (It also must be said that some adults have a double standard – accepting a level of chaos in their own areas of the house but nagging their offspring to keep to an unrealistic level of tidiness.)
- Set *some* limits – if piles of food-covered plates and dirty washing encourage vermin, reserve the right to call in a pest controller or industrial cleaner at their expense.

SIBLING RIVALRY

The constant teasing, bickering and competition that occurs between siblings can ramp up in the teenage years. A more colourful vocabulary and sophisticated tactics may mean that you are dealing with conflicts about different things and at a different level of intensity than in the early years. But dealt with in the right way, sibling rivalry can help your child learn about compromise, relating to peers, empathy and problem-solving.

What to do

- Focus on the content of the conflict, rather than who started it.
- Acknowledge your teenager's anger or resentment – these are valid emotions and demanding their suppression is not helpful. However, don't allow anger to spill over into cruel or dangerous behaviours. Help your daughter to understand that feelings and actions don't have to go together.
- Treat siblings as equals – make sure that one sibling isn't always benefited by the way a conflict is solved. Make sure that real compromise is achieved.
- Never compare siblings; for example, what subjects they excel at or at what age one achieved something that the other hasn't. Each is an individual, and your teenager will resent being evaluated only in relation to her sibling. Help your teenage siblings to set their own goals and expectations.
- Don't step in to solve the problem, unless mediation is necessary due to an unequal match of strength or eloquence. Listen to both sides of the story and help to broker a compromise.
- If, however, the intensity and frequency of the sibling squabbling becomes unbearable (or becomes physical or dangerous), you must intervene and, if you have no success in improving the situation, seek professional help.

CHORES AND POCKET MONEY

Contribution to household work is an important way to teach children what it means to belong to a family and a community. For this reason, chores should not be linked to pocket money or enforced with punishment. Being a contributing, trustworthy, reliable family member should not be offered as a choice, but rather communicated as an expectation. If chores are linked to pocket money and your daughter gets money in another way (gifts from relatives, part-time work) she can elect to forego the pay to avoid work. Contributing to the household should be presented as a message of mutual concern and shared responsibility. The best plan is to start early, ideally when children are very young. Trying to instigate new chore-related protocols after allowing young people to do nothing is fraught with difficulty, but is not impossible. And it is far better to try to instigate change than continue to do it all yourself.

What to do

- Sit down and talk through what needs to be done.
- Discuss what each of you think is reasonable for them to do in terms of what free time they have, what they are capable of and what they understand how to do.
- Give them a choice from a list that is drawn up.
- When you have agreed upon items from the list, put it up on the fridge.
- Perform the allocated task with them watching.
- Then watch while they do it, being very specific about what is required.

- Always enforce consequences if they forget – though be prepared to negotiate the completion time.
- Show appreciation once the job is done.
- Above all, don't do housework with resentment, reluctance or anger, otherwise you will teach your daughter to hate it, too.

PIERCINGS, PURPLE HAIR AND TATTOOS

As we have seen, identity development is a key developmental task in adolescence, and teenage girls will try on one 'mask' after another in order to find one that fits. For some girls this may involve pancake makeup; for others, blue hair and multiple piercings. Her reasons for wanting these body decorations may be due to peer pressure, a desire for rebellion, or both. But whatever the situation, unless her health is at risk, it is important not to criticise or judge.

Mouth piercings do carry health risks but these can be properly managed. Getting a GP to discuss the health risks with your daughter is a sensible option – these include infection (which can be serious, such as hepatitis C), thick scars or allergic reactions. There are jurisdictional differences in laws regarding both intimate (e.g. genitalia, anal region, nipples) and non-intimate (e.g. nose, tongue, face) piercings. In many states, it is illegal to perform an intimate piercing, even with parental consent, on a person under the age of 18 years. Some piercers may ask for parental consent if your daughter is under a certain age, even if the law in your area does not require this. If her school has a 'no tongue stud' or any similar rule then your daughter must obey that rule.

The same goes for coloured hair. Many of my teenage clients have elected to dye their hair and, when asked why, usually say something like: 'Changing my hair colour is important to me because I want to change something that isn't permanent. It's a way of expressing my emotions and myself.' If the school rules prohibit dyed hair, your daughter has no choice but to obey the rules. In the holidays, if she wishes to dye her hair to mimic an exotic Peruvian butterfly, then our advice is to let her go right ahead (with a non-permanent dye).

Tattoos are illegal for anyone under 18, but they are no longer the domain of pirates or prison inmates. They are increasingly common and complex, as seen on many celebrities, sports stars and everyday people. Despite the growing acceptance of tattoos, parents tend to have very mixed feelings. While some parents see it as a legitimate way for their daughter to express her individuality, others see it as a rebellious and immature act that carries significant health risks and will one day be regretted. Interestingly, in 1999 the American Academy of Child and Adolescent Psychiatry released a statement that listed tattooing as a possible form of self-injury.

A few years ago, I was asked to visit a school where a much-loved Year 12 student had died in an accident. The students in her sports team were united in their grief, and a few decided that to honour her memory they would get a tattoo of her face and name on their arm. Even though some of the students had reservations about this, the peer pressure was significant. The school asked me to chat with the bereaved teammates, and I began by mentioning the risks of tattooing if it wasn't done in a sterile environment (e.g. dirty needles passing infections such as hepatitis and HIV), that some of them might have allergies to various ink pigments, and that there was the side effect of unwanted scar tissue forming when getting a tattoo. I suggested that a compromise was that those in the team who wanted to could get a henna tattoo, which is a great option for those who don't want to commit to a permanent tattoo. I threw in that the FDA had not approved henna as a skin dye in the United States and that they should be aware of the possibilities of an allergic reaction. I concluded my state of the nation speech by letting them know, 'by the way', that henna can be dangerous to people with a G6PD deficiency, a condition where the body doesn't have enough of the enzyme glucose-6-phosphate dehydrogenase, which helps red blood cells function, so they should potentially check with their GP first. In the end, no one got a tattoo and instead they planted a tree in the school grounds in memory of their friend.

SLEEP

Sleep is the single most important behavioural experience your daughter can have. Research suggests that teenagers need at least nine hours' sleep a night, but in reality, the amount they get is often 5–7 hours. A sleep deficit can impact on a young person's attention and memory capacity, increase aggressive or withdrawn behaviours, and increase their risk of being overweight or obese. More seriously, sleep loss has been linked to an increased risk of depression, anxiety and drug abuse. Hectic schedules don't help, with after-school activities and sport, jobs and homework, and early school start times. But there is also a physiological basis – the delayed release of melatonin (the 'sleep-inducing' hormone) that occurs from puberty onwards means that teenagers don't feel sleepy until later in the evenings and delay bedtimes. The result? As many as 80 per cent of teenagers report being sleepy upon waking, which impacts their ability to function optimally at school.

There is a massive consensus among psychologists that sleep is without doubt the most important study skill going around. If your daughter does not have a good night's sleep after studying, her ability to retain the information she has studied is enormously diminished. However, sleep does much more than just help in the consolidation and retrieval of memories. Research has found that a teenager's ability to come up with novel solutions to complex problems is greatly enhanced by a good night's sleep. In fact, it's been calculated to give her a threefold boost. Sleeping at night also enriches her creativity, as new neural pathways are forged and less important ones fade away.

What to do

- Make sure the room is cool, dark and quiet.
- Enforce a 'no technology' rule in the bedroom.

Back-lit screens can interfere with melatonin production, so all devices need to be switched off one hour before bed and put on charge in a public space.

- Encourage some wind-down time before bed. Tackling that really hard maths problem then falling into bed is going to be less sleep friendly than a quiet period of reading or listening to music.

- Encourage your child to keep regular sleep and wake times, and to fall asleep in bed (rather than on the couch).

- Don't offer caffeinated drinks, including energy drinks, cola or coffee, within six hours of bedtime.

Be aware that sleep problems can be a sign of mental health problems. For example, young people with anxiety often have difficulty falling asleep and those with depression may wake up during the night and be unable to fall back asleep. Consult with your GP if you are worried.

I'm sick of having to wake my daughter up every morning so she can get to school on time. She's always got an excuse about forgetting to set her alarm or sleeping through it. What should I do?

Biological sleep patterns during adolescence do make it difficult for girls to get to sleep before 11 p.m., but just because a girl's biology doesn't match up with the demands of the outside world doesn't mean that you have to surrender to the daily insanity of getting her up and out of the house. Teenage girls need to understand that their choices have consequences. Never do anything for teenage girls that they can do for themselves. Sit down with your daughter and have a discussion about getting up in the morning. You might say, 'You and I have a hard time in the morning. I am no longer going to be responsible for getting you up on time. I will give you one wake up call, and then it's up to you. If you miss the bus, I will not drive you to school. You will need to either find another way to get there, or you will need to call school and face the consequences.'

NUTRITION

Breakfast is the most important meal of the day, especially for adolescents, who need the energy to concentrate at school. A UK study reported that 39 per cent of girls skipped breakfast some or all of the time, with many of them wrongly believing that it would help them lose weight. Children who miss breakfast are more likely to snack on sugary foods later in the day, and are at risk of diabetes later in life. Many also experience difficulty concentrating in lessons, and become lethargic and exhibit behavioural problems. Breakfast, like sleep, is an issue that must be non-negotiable. Princess B is likely to resist this, as peer pressure is often focused on weight reduction.

Another issue is encouraging young people to eat plenty of fresh vegetables, fruit and unprocessed grains and to steer clear of sugary, processed foods. This can be a challenge if their peers eat piles of junk food, but if you have started early your child will hopefully have a good understanding of why eating healthy food is important.

Parents also need to be aware of the importance of brain-derived neurotrophic factor (BDNF), which is a protein that can be thought of as a 'brain fertiliser'. It helps the brain develop new connections, as discussed in chapter 2, repair damaged brain cells and protect the brain from neurodegenerative diseases such as Alzheimer's disease. Exercise can raise levels of BDNF, as does a healthy diet, but sugar and processed foods can do the exact opposite. Research by academics such as Associate Professor Felice Jacka, well known for her work that focuses on links between diet and mental health, suggests that individuals who eat a BDNF-rich diet, such as the Mediterranean diet (high in plant-based foods, whole grains, legumes and nuts), report lower levels of depressive symptoms and higher levels of wellbeing.

It can also be difficult when your daughter has started to use food to distract herself from emotional problems (some people call this emotional eating). When we feel anxious or depressed, many of us look to food (especially sugary or fatty foods) to make us feel better. And there is a biological reason for this. Sweet foods activate the reward pathways in our brains, which makes sense because our brains run on glucose and we need it for all of our bodily functions. However, when we have too much sugar, it not only gets stored as fat (hello heart disease), but also messes with our insulin levels (insulin resistance), which can lead to type 2 diabetes.

As mentioned, a healthy relationship with food begins when children are very young. But it is never too late to introduce good eating habits, even if in the teenage years you may be modelling good habits rather than implementing them. The following strategies may help to change the way food and nutrition are viewed in your home.

What to do

- Kick the nightly dessert habit. By using dessert as a reward for eating a healthy dinner, you are sending the message that nutritious food is inferior to sugary food. Make dessert an occasional treat.

- Avoid using sweets or junk food as a reward for good behaviour – it creates an unhealthy relationship with food that can easily tip over into addictive behaviour when they experience stress.

- Avoid simply admonishing your teen if they make unhealthy food choices. Explain why their choice could be better, and avoid explanations that simply label something as 'fattening'. For example, describe how foods high in sugar leave you craving more, creating an unhealthy vicious circle of consumption.

- Provide easy-to-eat options, such as cherry tomatoes, grapes, tubs of yoghurt and cheese cubes. These are great 'on the run' healthy foods for busy teenagers.

- Rather than having a bowl of salad or vegetables in the middle of the table at meal time, make sure everyone has a serve on their plate at the start of the meal. They will see it as a normal part of the meal and will be more likely to eat it.

- Children's palates develop at different rates. Continue to offer children and teenagers a range of different foods, as it may take a number of exposures to the food before they like it. Don't assume that because your child didn't eat something in the early years, they still won't eat it in the teen years. You may be pleasantly surprised.

- Purchase fresh fruit and vegetables in season and talk about how they will taste better than out-of-season produce. See Nutrition Australia's website for more information.
- Encourage teens to look for recipes online, then shop for ingredients and cook them together. Talk about the ingredients and encourage them to find recipes that have a good balance of nutrients.
- Look for holiday program activities that focus on cooking and nutrition.
- Most importantly, model healthy eating habits yourself.

If you have teenagers who still hate vegetables and prefer junk food, don't despair. As mentioned in chapter 2, teenagers often aren't yet capable of understanding future consequences of current behaviours, so the idea of eating healthily so as not to get sick later in life is irrelevant to them. As their brains mature, their tastes in food will likely mature as well. Continue to model good choices and provide healthy options, and the rest will fall into place.

CURFEWS

Setting a time for when you want your teenager home can be a major headache for parents. The American

Academy of Pediatrics (AAP) recommends 7–8 p.m. for young teenagers (12–13 years) and 8–9 p.m. for middle adolescents (14–15 years). The trick is to enter into reasonable negotiations with your daughter as she grows, as experience suggests that this is associated with greater compliance. Many experts recommend curfews because they set clear boundaries for your teen. Your expectations should be realistic and based on the event itself. Be rational and reasonable.

> My daughter is in Year 9 and wants to go to a party with her boyfriend (he's in Year 10). I know where the party is and that there will be adult supervision, but I still want her home at a reasonable hour. How should I handle this?

As with any boundary, discuss what's safe and fair *before* she goes, and decide on a reasonable consequence if she's late. One size does not fit all, and if you believe that your daughter can keep herself safe, hangs out with others who also engage in safe behaviours and is not likely to engage in sensation seeking, then you may be more inclined to give her some space. If she does seriously stuff up and breaches your trust, try not to let your first reaction be one of anger and betrayal. It's important to remember that this is really not about you. Even though it often feels personal, it's not a reflection on you or your parenting. Instead, take action and help her learn how to take responsibility. It's important not to enable your daughter by blaming others or minimising the problem, such as: 'The other kids talked her into it.' Remember, if you give in and enable your daughter, you'll be teaching her not to take responsibility, setting her up for problems down the road.

TECHNOLOGY

Unless you are living under the proverbial rock, arguments around technology are likely to feature often in your family. The difficult part is that most of us don't yet know the effects that 24/7 access to information, news and social groups may have on our teenagers. And this means we stumble over, deflect or make a substantial effort to ignore the problems that technology won't always, but can, cause.

In a 2015 study by the American Psychological Association, it was found that girls are more likely to be negatively affected academically by compulsive texting behaviours than boys. The reason may lie in gender differences regarding why teens text. Previous research shows that teen boys use digital technology to convey information, while girls use it for social interaction and to nurture relationships. Teenage girls are also more likely than boys to ruminate with others, or engage in obsessive, preoccupied thinking across contexts. Therefore, it may be that the nature of the texts girls send and receive means they are more distracting, thus interfering with their academic adjustment. Parents need to talk to their children early on about treating people with respect when texting and never writing anything that they would not want the four Ps to see – parents, police, the school principal or a paedophile.

My suggestion? Teenagers can have privacy in their bedrooms, or access to the internet, but they can't have both. The internet is a public place – which means it is used in a public area, such as the lounge room. For young users who are yet to fully find their digital feet, their use of the internet should be conditional on the premise that they will show you, whenever asked, what they are doing. Trust needs to be built – it is not an automatic right.

What to do

- Set clear boundaries around technology use.
  For primary school children, one hour of screen entertainment is enough each day, moving to two hours in early secondary school. Set a time at night when all devices are on charge or locked away in a public room in the house. No phones should be in use when homework is being done.
- Encourage and initiate activities that don't use a screen, especially outdoors.
- Consider the extent to which your daughter's friendships online are important to her. Social media can keep kids connected to people who value and support them. It's not all bad – but encourage offline friendships as well.
- Encourage your child to always engage in respectful relationships online.
- Don't think that avoiding giving your daughter access to her own social networking accounts, such as Instagram and Facebook, will mean she won't

experience cyber bullying. She may get talked about anyway – and this may travel into the schoolyard.

- For younger adolescents (tweens) there are simple tools that can be used to enforce the boundaries you set. Free software programs like Our Pact, Cold Turkey and Self Control allow you to block out, for a set time, websites that your daughter may gravitate to for distraction, allowing her to stay focused on things like homework or chores. There are also random wi-fi password generators that change every day, enabling parents to regulate access to the net each day: 'You can have today's password when you make your bed, do your allocated chore and walk the dog!' This is a great way for your teen to learn that she must do what she needs to do before doing what she wants to do.
- For older adolescents, don't rely on filters to do the job! You need to monitor your child's use regularly. Smart kids will work around filters in a flash and Princess B is very cyber savvy.

Before we move on, let's just remind ourselves that adolescence is usually just a stage, like toddler tantrums. The reason that adolescence is harder to handle is the volatile mix of factors we looked at earlier (the mismatch of physical and mental development, peer pressure, social media influences, lack of confidence among parents who feel guilty about being time poor, etc.). The best way forward is for parents to learn to gradually give up control to its rightful owner, and for the young woman to learn to accept this responsibility without abusing it. However unlikely it may seem at times, the fact is that this emotional battle of wills will come to a natural, healthy end as your girl is replaced by the fine young woman she is destined to become.

However, for a small number of teenagers, adolescence is the time of onset for mental health problems (see chapter 15). If you are in any doubt as to whether or not your daughter's behaviour is normal, make a time to talk to your GP.

Chapter 11

Sex matters

It is time to acknowledge that your daughter is a sexual being (and has been for a while – we are actually sexual beings from the womb to the tomb). Parents may find this development in adolescence eye-poppingly speedy, but it's critical that you keep up with what's going on.

The 2013 National Survey of Australian Secondary Students and Sexual Health showed that by Year 10, around one-quarter of Australian teens have had sexual intercourse, rising to around one-half in Year 12. Almost a quarter of sexually active students had sex with three or more people in the past year. The survey revealed an association between alcohol and other drugs and sex, with almost one in seven young women reporting being drunk or high the last time they had sex. More than one-quarter of girls reported having sex when they didn't want to; of these, half cited being too drunk as a reason, and almost one fifth as being too 'high'.

The good news is that many young women cite their mums as among the most useful sources of information, which has been the case for years. But there's also a big new player in the game of sex education – technology. If most episodes of *Keeping Up With the Kardashians* leave you wanting to cover your daughter's eyes and ears, realise that this is just a tiny, and very tame, glimpse into what is available online and shared by young people. According to the same survey, the impact of technology on the sexual behaviours of girls is abundantly clear. More than half (54 per cent) of girls had received a sexually explicit text, and 41 per cent had sent one. One in four girls had sent a sexually explicit nude or nearly nude photo or video of themselves. When the researchers just looked at the situation for those girls who were sexually active, the figures for receiving and sending an explicit text jumped to 85 per cent and 70 per cent – and half of these girls had sent a sexually explicit nude or nearly nude photo or video of themselves.

According to cyber safety expert Susan McLean, the average age at which young people first see online pornography in Australia is eleven years of age. If pornographic and other sexualised images are routinely viewed by young people, it can lead to the reinforcement of harmful gender stereotypes, contribute to young people forming unhealthy and sexist views of women and sex, and may contribute to condoning violence against women and normalising sexual violence and sexually coercive behaviour.

As in most situations, open, honest and frank communication with your daughter is the key. Never miss an opportunity to talk with your daughter about sex from the earliest time – many girls gradually become more self-conscious each year, so the earlier you start talking, the better. Remember, research also tells us that girls who feel that they can talk about sex with their parents – because their parents speak willingly and listen carefully to them – are less likely to engage in risky behaviours than those who feel they can't discuss these things at home. An uncomfortable moment in a movie could lead to a great discussion about puberty, peer pressure or even love; a news item might raise the topic of links between drug use and unsafe sex. So take a deep breath and dive in . . .

What to do

- Don't wait for your daughter to bring the subject up. If you say nothing, she may conclude that you are unapproachable. Plan to start the conversations about sex yourself.
- Share your values, beliefs and attitudes about sex with your daughter. She needs help to develop a values framework from which to make and stand by good decisions.
- Learn as much as you can about issues of sex and sexuality, so that you can answer questions accurately and openly. Your daughter should know about all the predictable topics, such as puberty, menstruation, reproduction and contraception, but she also wants to hear about things like how to have a loving, intimate and good quality relationship, and how to say no under pressure. The more you know, the less you will stumble.

- Practise what you plan to say, and how you say it, with your partner or friends. Many parents feel uncomfortable talking to their children about sexual matters. Try the words out so you feel comfortable with them and can convey them in an understandable way.
- Make sex a regular and ongoing topic of conversation, rather than a big one-off talk. Aim for a friendly two-way chat, not a lecture. Ask what she thinks and feels, and try to get a lively conversation going.
- Have back-up information available. Look for books such as *Girl Stuff* by Kaz Cooke, and good quality articles in magazines such as *Girlfriend* or online.
- Educate yourself about the prevalence and use of online pornography, and how it impacts on young people's understanding of sex and relationships. It is almost certain that your child will be exposed to online pornography, either intentionally or unintentionally, and often at a young age. The website 'It's time we talked' (itstimewetalked. com.au) has great resources for parents and young people about pornography.
- Make a connection between sex, love and intimacy. Use family events, such as a wedding or a birth, to discuss love and responsibility to others.
- Respect your daughter's growing need for privacy. Most become extremely embarrassed about nakedness (yours as well as their own).

- Demonstrate that you trust your daughter to behave responsibly in sexual matters. This should act as an incentive for her to live up to your expectations. Constant prying or suspicion will have the opposite effect.
- Give clear information about behaviour that's appropriate in any sexual situations – emphasising that her body is private and no one has the right to do anything she doesn't want or to make her feel uncomfortable. Giving your daughter this information early means that she'll be less vulnerable to abuse.
- Don't mock her crushes.
- Don't rely on the school, friends or the internet to be a good source of truthful information. Around half of young people find school sex education irrelevant or lacking. You can be instrumental in filling the gaps.

SAME-SEX ATTRACTION

It is normal for young people to experiment with sexual identities. Some will feel certain quite early that they are attracted to people of the same sex, while others may question and experiment for years. In the 2013 National Survey of Australian Secondary Students and Sexual Health, around 4 per cent of young women were attracted only to people of the same sex, 15 per cent were attracted to both sexes, and around 5 per cent were unsure.

Despite great advances in community education, it is unfortunate that homophobia, transphobia and the belief that people fall into distinct gender roles (man and woman; otherwise known as heteronormativity) are still rife in Australia, and can have a serious impact on the health and wellbeing of young people who are gender variant or sexuality diverse. Sadly, LGBTIQ (lesbian, gay, bisexual, transgender, intersex and questioning) young people are six times more likely to take their own lives in comparison to other young people. According to a 2014 study of LGBTIQ by the Young and Well CRC, 41 per cent of respondents had thought about self-harm and/or suicide, 33 per cent had harmed themselves, and 16 per cent had attempted suicide.

Since health and wellbeing outcomes for same-sex-attracted young people are often poorer than others, it is very important to create a safe space for your daughter (or her friends) to discuss these issues with you.

What to do

- Be supportive and let her know that you love her for exactly who she is, no matter what.
- If it comes as a shock, stay calm and acknowledge how great it is that your daughter has confided in you. This is about your daughter, not you.
- Explore whether she has faced any issues around bullying or personal safety, especially at school, and encourage her to seek support.
- Look for useful resources, for both you and your daughter (see Resources).

- Avoid asking her lots of intrusive questions. She may need to spend some time exploring what it means to be same-sex-attracted before she can discuss it in any detail.
- If you are really struggling with the idea, tell her that you need a little time to process what she is telling you. Make sure you set a time with her to come back to the discussion, and stick to it. Consider involving a third party, such as a qualified counsellor who has experience working with same-sex-attracted teenagers.

Chapter 12

Bullying

Despite concerted public education programs, many parents still misunderstand what is meant by the word bullying. If a girl comes home and says that X doesn't like her or doesn't agree with her – that is NOT bullying. If she says she was not invited to a party or picked for a team – that is NOT bullying. Bullying is deliberate and repeated harassment (verbal, physical, social or psychological aggression) with the intention to cause harm.

Psychologists describe the chief form of bullying in Girl World as 'relational aggression'. It is based firmly in cliques (see page 42) and simply means the ways in which girls manipulate the social scene to hurt selected peers. Spreading rumours, telling lies, revealing secrets and 'the silent treatment' are all forms of relational aggression – and nothing in history has provided a greater hotbed for this than the internet and social media. This sort of psychological cruelty has both short- and long-term consequences.

When I talk to adolescent girls about the experience of being bullied, I often ask them what they wished their parents had done to make their lives easier at the time. Many have told me that they wished their parents had taken their concerns seriously instead of minimising and trivialising their pain with comments such as, 'It's just a phase – it will pass' or 'She's just jealous'.

These girls wanted someone to name the nature and extent of the loss, to honour their pain for what it was – disturbing, distressing and shattering. It's hard for parents to just listen and hold their daughters, but that's exactly what these girls say they wanted. The trouble is that research suggests one in two victims will tell no one.

HOW TO TELL IF YOUR DAUGHTER IS BEING BULLIED

The privacy afforded by mobile and internet technology can make it more difficult to know when your child is being bullied. (It's not always like the old days when kids came home with black eyes, torn clothing or missing books.)

However, like any abuse, it can have various effects on young people, including poor performance at school, feelings of sadness, physical illness and lower self-esteem. Combined with other factors in the young person's life, cyber bullying can sometimes lead to serious mental health issues such as anxiety disorders and depression, and may even lead to self-harm and suicide.

Some signs to look out for include:

- changing patterns of internet or mobile phone use
- receiving more-frequent text messages or ones at odd hours of the day or night
- having nightmares or trouble sleeping
- becoming withdrawn and not socialising with friends
- feeling unwell and not wanting to go to school.

Recognising these signs will assist you in helping your daughter deal with the bullying and to develop strategies to cope.

What to do

- Ask her about her relationships with others, and then be quiet and pay attention. Reflect back to her what you hear, confirming it with statements such as, 'Lisa's been your best friend for so long. That must have hurt.' Show your empathy by sharing your own stories and experiences.
- If she rejects your overtures, persist in asking questions (not immediately, give her a break!). And don't take dismissals personally ('What would you know?' or 'I don't care anyway') – she may simply be trying to dull the pain. Keep asking questions, and stay connected.
- Offer help if she wants it. If, for example, she is being picked on as she walks home alone, help her identify some friends who she can walk with. If she wants to confront her aggressor, discuss the best way to do it (pick a time when they are alone,

not with friends) and role-play it a couple of times. If she is being cyber bullied, tell her to stop the correspondence immediately and block the cyber bully.

- Practise assertiveness with her. One of the best ways to stop gossip is to confront it early. Suggest that your daughter approach someone who is spreading gossip and say something like, 'I don't know if this is true, but I heard that you said this about me, and I want it to stop.' Practise it with her before she does so.

- Encourage her to find her spark (see page 97). Girls who excel in some arena, whether it is sport, art, academic studies, music, drama or another field, are less susceptible to aggression than other girls. Self-esteem doesn't drop from the sky – they get it by being good at things.

- Help her examine the habit of gossip. How long can she go without gossiping? Could she and her friends journal their gossiping? Who gossips the most? This is both tangible and eye opening to adolescents. It is also a way of recording abuse.

- Encourage her to stand up for victims by refusing to be an 'audience' for a bully. She does not need to publicly challenge the bully, but to simply walk away (or if the abuse is online, she can refuse to participate). Once people stop participating, the dynamics change – often the abuse just dies off.

- Don't trivialise her pain. Comments like, 'It was probably just a joke' or 'She can't be a real friend if she behaves like that' all miss the point. They only prove to your daughter how out of touch you are.

- Don't intervene by contacting the bully's parents. This is sure to embarrass her and suggests that you don't have confidence in her ability to handle things herself. If you must intervene, begin discreetly, maybe with someone at her school who you are comfortable approaching (see below).
- Don't make restrictions on her use of technology if she is being cyber bullied. Discuss ways of dealing with cyber bullies and talk with the school if necessary. If you restrict her use of technology, this may backfire – the online social world is as important as the offline one, and she may opt to not tell you in future if the consequence will be staying offline.

Approaching school when your daughter is being bullied

This is not easy, not least because describing events second hand is difficult, particularly since most of these acts are subtle and indirect forms of aggression. In addition, many parents find it difficult to express their concerns and tend to be either very apologetic or too aggressive. They may also engage in character assassination of the young people in question, rather than focusing on their behaviour. It is all too easy in such situations to be labelled a hysterical parent who is overreacting to her daughter's social shortcomings. A smarter approach is to document your concerns via an email to the teacher, copied to the year level coordinator and/or deputy principal, with a request to meet. At the meeting, calmly discuss with the teacher your concerns about what is happening, and ascertain whether they are aware of the interaction and the impact on the victim. If the situation continues after the meeting, seek a discussion with someone with more authority. Among other things, ask if your daughter can switch classes, because a great deal of social chemistry, particularly in schools, forms along classroom lines.

Chapter 13

Alcohol

Binge-drinking among young people is very common, and is considered by most young people to be a rite of passage in their teenage years. Princess B's parents, along with many others, have probably never heard of the National Health and Medical Research Council (NHMRC), Australia's leading expert body that, among other roles, develops evidence-based health advice for communities and professionals. In 2009 the NHMRC, using evidence to make an assessment of the potential alcohol-related harms (such as injury and disease) that people may experience from drinking, published Guidelines to Reduce Health Risks from Drinking Alcohol. These guidelines recommend that *children and young people under the age of 18 do not drink*. They based their recommendations on the fact that young people's brains are still developing and that drinking alcohol during this time may damage their brain and lead to health complications later in life.

While several parts of the brain are affected by alcohol during the teenage years, there are two particularly sensitive areas: the hippocampus and the prefrontal lobe. Heavy and extended alcohol use in adolescence has been associated with a reduction in the hippocampal volume, which is responsible for memory and learning. The prefrontal lobe, which undergoes the most intensive changes in adolescence, is important for planning, judgement, decision-making, impulse control and language. Adolescents who drink heavily have smaller prefrontal lobes than non-drinkers of the same age.

Recently introduced legislation in Victoria means that it is against the law to serve alcohol in a private home to any person under 18, unless that person has written permission from a parent or guardian. This law is part of an effort to reduce the harm of drinking for young people and their families and friends. Indeed, the research is clear that the earlier Princess B is introduced to alcohol, the more likely she is to develop problems with it later in life.

One of the great fears of any parent of a teenage girl is that their daughter will become involved in and/ or dependent on alcohol, cigarettes or other drugs. The good news is that the National Drug Strategy Household Survey in 2013 showed that young people are delaying starting smoking, and the number who smoke regularly is decreasing each year – daily smoking rates have almost halved since 1991. Similarly, the study found that fewer teenagers aged 12–17 were drinking alcohol and continued to delay starting drinking. The age at which 14–24-year-olds first tried alcohol increased from 14.4 years in 1998 to 15.7 years in 2013. However, considering that the NHMRC recommend that children and young people under the age of 18 don't drink *at all*, there are still too many adolescents drinking at risky levels.

My clinical experience is that Princess B and her friends should therefore delay their first drink for as long as possible. While young people are influenced by the internet, peers and siblings, parents continue to be the greatest influence (even though it may not feel like it). Research indicates that a majority (86 per cent) of young people are willing to talk to their parents about the harms associated with alcohol, and three-quarters (74 per cent) say their parents could influence their drinking habits.

Many health professionals believe that girls who feel good about themselves are less likely to consume alcohol. In contrast, the more miserable young people are, the more likely they are to abuse alcohol and other drugs as a form of self-medication – in other words, to drown their psychological pain. Helping your daughter find her spark, and encouraging her relationships with positive role models is an important part of helping her develop resistance to the many pressures she will face in the teenage years.

What to do

- Lead by example. Some 60 per cent of young people say that their parents are the chief influence on whether they drink or not, and parents who drink are more likely to have children who take up the habit.
- Don't be moralistic. Preaching and trying to control your daughter tends to inspire rebellion. Instead,

talk to her about how to deal with peer pressure about drinking alcohol.

- Don't condone regular drinking in the first three years of high school, and try to delay drinking for as long as possible thereafter.
- Don't panic if she comes home drunk. Ensure her physical safety and help her recover. Remember that recovery takes time. Studies indicate that about 10 per cent of the alcohol in a beverage leaves the body in breath, sweat and urine, but the liver has to break down the other 90 per cent, at a rate of *one standard drink per hour*. None of the conventional 'sobering up' myths can speed this up – not black coffee, cold showers, exercise or vomiting.
- Don't try to engage in conversation if your daughter is affected by alcohol. Wait until she sobers up, and then get the facts.
- Don't hesitate to let her know you don't approve, and that if this becomes a regular pattern you will take her to get professional help, starting with a visit to your GP.

DRINK SPIKING

Drink spiking is a serious and illegal behaviour that has been associated with sexual assaults and deaths. While it is hard to estimate the extent of drink spiking, mainly due to underreporting, one study has estimated that up to 4000 incidents in Australia occurred in a twelve-month period (with around 4 in 5 victims being women and half under the age of 24 years), with approximately one-third of these leading to sexual assault.

Ways to minimise the possibility of drink spiking that you can discuss with your daughter include:

- Don't accept drinks from strangers or leave drinks unattended.
- Always watch what is happening if others are preparing your drink, including bartenders.
- Don't drink anything that you didn't see opened or didn't open yourself.
- Leave your drink unfinished if you are unsure it is okay, or if it tastes funny.
- Party in a group and watch out for each other.
- If you feel dizzy or sick, ask someone you trust to take you somewhere safe.
- If you are alone or can't find your friends, tell the staff behind the bar.
- If someone collapses and/or is unconscious, call an ambulance immediately and don't leave them alone.
- If you are on a date with someone you don't know, meet in a public space and arrange your own transport to and from the venue. Arrange for a friend to call you at some stage of the evening and/ or pick you up.

See www.betterhealth.vic.gov.au/health/healthyliving/ drink-spiking for further information.

Chapter 14

Illegal drugs

Many parents, not surprisingly, are frightened and confused about illicit drugs. Media coverage of the issue is nearly always alarmist and inflammatory, serving only to increase everyone's anxiety levels. As parents, it is our role and responsibility to pass on accurate and up-to-date information about drugs to our children, and the only way to do this is to do our research. The Alcohol and Drug Foundation (ADF) website (www.druginfo.adf.org.au) provides accurate, reliable and up-to-date information for parents.

The ADF estimates that, in terms of illicit drugs, around one in six young people aged 12–17 years has tried inhalants (17 per cent); one in seven has tried cannabis (15 per cent), and a significant minority have tried hallucinogens (3 per cent), amphetamines (2.9 per cent), ecstasy (2.7 per cent), steroids (2 per cent), cocaine (1.7 per cent) and heroin (1.6 per cent).

These drugs are illegal for good reason, and are especially dangerous for young people who, as we have seen, are undergoing a unique period in neurodevelopment. Research has indicated that substance use in adolescence impacts on the developing brain, and scans show abnormalities in brain functioning that are linked to long-term changes in cognition. Abnormalities have also been seen in brain structure, brain volume and the quality of 'white matter'.

Despite the fact that many girls have said that cannabis is 'great', helps them to relax and should be one of the essential food groups, in the short term, marijuana use has been shown to impair attention, memory, learning and decision-making, and those effects can last for days after the high wears off. I often have to send cannabis users a 2014 study into the long-term effects of cannabis use, which demolishes the argument that the drug is safe. The study, by Professor Wayne Hall (an Australian researcher who advises the World Health Organization), builds a compelling case against those who deny the devastation that cannabis wreaks on the brain. Professor Hall found that cannabis is highly addictive, causes mental health problems and opens the door to hard drugs.

Amphetamines such as ice have dominated media stories in recent times. The final report of the National Ice Taskforce, released in 2015, reported that Australians use proportionately more methamphetamine than almost all other countries, and its use is growing. The report indicated that over 200 000 Australians reported using the crystalline form of methamphetamine (commonly known as ice) in 2013, in comparison to less than 100 000 in 2007. These figures are seen as conservative and already dated. The report further notes that ice is an extremely powerful stimulant, unlike cannabis and heroin, which are depressants. Stimulants speed up the communication between the brain and the central nervous system, which increases alertness and physical activity. They are well known as party drugs as a result. However, for some people this manifests in psychological disturbances or violent behaviours. Long-term, the drug causes impaired attention, memory and motor skills. The report concludes that the distress that ice use causes for individuals, families, communities and frontline workers is far worse than other drugs.

There remains a strong market for ice at the time of writing this book. It is easy to obtain and relatively cheap compared to other drugs. One of the concerning findings of the taskforce was that, despite efforts by law enforcement agencies to prevent supply, there has been little response in the market. Even large seizures of product have failed to push up the cost of the drug, which should occur if demand is strong.

Some experts suggest that the use of recreational drugs by young people who are genetically predisposed to mental health problems is responsible not only for an increase in the prevalence of these disorders, but also for the fact that they are occurring at a much younger age.

Isobel is 17 and lives with her parents. She dropped out of school a year ago and is now doing a pre-apprenticeship in hairdressing. Every Friday she goes nightclubbing with friends, getting home in the early hours of Saturday morning, by which time she is often drunk and drug-affected. She doesn't help at all around the house and has begun skipping classes at TAFE. On the few occasions that her father has tried to reason with her, she has withdrawn to her room to put on a 'floorshow' of anger and abuse or run away to her boyfriend's place. Her personality seems to be changing and her mother, who hates conflict, begs her father not to confront her.

If Isobel continues to refuse her parents' reasonable requests to share the household chores, return from clubbing at a reasonable hour and stop her illegal behaviours (underage drinking and illegal drug use) then it is perfectly acceptable for her parents to grab the parenting reins. First, they should remove the privileges that Isobel takes for granted (access to TV, internet and family car, and/ or having her mobile phone bill paid) until she complies with her parents' requests. There is bound to be a standoff, especially if their parenting has been inconsistent in the past. But, if they do nothing, they are in effect supporting Isobel's lifestyle. On the other hand, intervening may help her get her life back on track.

Even if, as can happen in extreme cases, Isobel threatens violence or damages property as a response to the interventions, her parents must not back down. They should issue a warning that any violent behaviours will result in the police being called and, if the behaviour continues, follow through. Parenting is about preparing our offspring for the world and Isobel must learn that behaving in a socially unacceptable way has societal consequences. I recognise this may be a very hard thing for parents to enact – seek help from resources like parenting help lines if necessary (see the Resources section).

What to do

- Find out as much as you can about drugs and alcohol from a reliable up-to-date source.
- Approach the topic rationally rather than emotionally. Harm minimisation (that is, safe use of drugs) is a more realistic approach than zero tolerance. As we have seen, at this stage of her life a blanket ban is unlikely to work.
- Lead by example. As mentioned in the section on alcohol, more than half of young people say that their parents are the primary influence on whether they drink or not. This also applies to the use of illicit drugs.
- Help her to avoid people and places that may be avenues of introduction for drug use.
- Don't be moralistic. Preaching and trying to control will only fuel rebellion. Instead, talk to her about how she may respond if someone offers her drugs.
- Don't panic if she comes home drug-affected. Ensure her physical safety and help her recover. It may take some hours for the effects of the drug to wear off. The effects of ice, for example, can last for around six hours.
- Don't try to engage in conversation if your daughter is affected by alcohol or drugs. Wait until she sobers

up, and then get the facts.
- Don't hesitate to let her know you don't approve, and that if this becomes a regular pattern you will take her to get professional help, starting with a visit to your GP.

Chapter 15
Mental health

Although it's a cliché to talk about 'teen angst', many parents still find it hard to deal with their daughters' often intense emotions, which is one reason they drop the ball when it comes to setting and enforcing boundaries. The danger here is that parents may be ignoring signs of a developing mental illness, which can have similar symptoms to what are commonly thought of as normal teenage mood swings. Many parents I see in clinical practice compare their teenager's behaviours to their own at a similar age. This strategy can be unhelpful for many reasons, the most important one being that times have changed. The reality is that much behaviour initiated in the teenage years, such as experimenting with sexual behaviours and drugs or alcohol, occurs at a considerably earlier age than in previous generations.

If all of your teenager's friends and classmates are already engaging in this type of behaviour then, whether you approve of it or not, you will know that this behaviour is 'normal', and there is less of a possibility that mental illness is present. If you discover that your daughter is *way* outside the bell curve, then you may have reason for concern.

The age of onset for the vast majority of mental health problems in young women is 24, and half begin before the age of 15. Put simply, adolescence is a giant Petri dish in which the seeds are sown for either a good mental health trajectory or a really lousy one. Which way they develop is due to a mixture of genetics, personality, temperament, upbringing and the delicate balance of risk and protective factors in their environment.

So what are some of the signs to look for?

- Decrease in enjoyment and time spent with family and friends
- Significant decrease in school performance
- Strong resistance to attending school, or absenteeism
- Problems with memory, attention or concentration
- Significant changes in energy levels, eating or sleeping patterns
- Physical symptoms, e.g. stomach-aches, headaches, backaches
- Feelings of hopelessness, sadness or anxiety or frequent crying
- Frequent aggression, disobedience or verbal lashing out
- Excessive neglect of personal appearance or hygiene
- Substance abuse
- Dangerous or illegal thrill-seeking behaviour

- Being overly suspicious of others
- Seeing or hearing things that others do not

I must stress that the presence of these behaviours and/or symptoms does not necessarily imply a young person is mentally ill. I list them here so that parents are more able to recognise them, and to judge to what extent they are interfering with the key developmental tasks of adolescence, which are:

- making friends
- figuring out who they are
- emancipating from parents
- functioning at school and acquiring the skills for future independence.

If even *one* of these developmental tasks is significantly disrupted due to the behaviours and symptoms described above, then help must be sought from your doctor or nearest mental health service, such as headspace.

The most crucial warning signs of mental distress or illness are social withdrawal, loss of interest in things that used to be pleasurable, trouble sleeping, decreased appetite and/or changes in energy levels. These behaviours may be a temporary response to a minor setback, such as a particularly bad week, a romantic breakup or not making the netball team. The behaviours are more likely to be important and require help if they last longer than a couple of weeks and impact on your daughter's ability to function normally.

A major challenge is encouraging young people to seek help, as illustrated by a 2015 UK study by the National Union of Students. Of the 1093 students in further and higher education who were surveyed, 78 per cent said they experienced mental health issues in the last year, and over half of these students said they did not seek support. A third said they would not know where to get mental health support at their college or university if they needed it, and 40 per cent reported being nervous about the support they would receive from their institution.

ANXIETY

Thirty years ago, anxiety disorders such as obsessive compulsive disorder (OCD) or generalised anxiety disorder (GAD) in young people were almost unheard of. The most recent national survey of mental health disorders in children and adolescents, published in 2015, showed that 7 per cent of young people aged 12–17 had been diagnosed with an anxiety disorder and that the figures were higher for young women (7.7 per cent compared to 6.3 per cent for boys).

Anxiety is a normal response to something that is terrifying or complicated. Adrenaline flows into the bloodstream, priming muscles, focusing attention, flooding the body with oxygen and releasing chemicals that transform the sugar in the bloodstream into energy. This 'fight or flight' response happens to everyone faced with a difficult situation. Originally named for its ability to enable us to physically fight or run away when faced with danger, it is now activated in situations where neither response is appropriate, such as being stuck in traffic or during a stressful day at work. When the perceived threat is gone, systems are designed to return to normal functioning via the relaxation response, but in times of chronic stress this fails to happen often enough, causing damage to the body. The bottom line is that some teenagers can get caught in fight or flight mode, and anxiety can start to take over their lives.

Anxiety warning signs

- Feeling a constant sense of dread that something terrible will happen
- Having trouble falling asleep
- Having difficulty concentrating or thinking straight
- Experiencing physical symptoms such as nausea, chest pain, involuntary shaking, increased sweating, difficulty breathing or a racing heart (panic attacks)
- Displaying avoidance behaviours (e.g. refusing to go out), or repetitive or obsessive behaviours

What to do

- Engage your daughter in conversation:
  Do you ever feel like your heart is going to jump out of your chest or that you can't breathe?
  Do you ever feel that something terrible is going to happen even when you are safe?'
- Listen carefully to what she says. If she has had panic attacks, or is starting to feel a constant sense of dread even when she's safe, it's important to get professional face-to-face help. Take her to your

GP and arrange to see a psychologist trained in cognitive behavioural therapy (which has a good success rate for anxiety treatment). If you don't get help, your daughter may eventually become so anxious about being anxious that she won't leave home in case she can't cope with her anxiety in public. This is panic disorder.

- Find out everything you can about anxiety (see Resources).
- Encourage your daughter to exercise and to avoid caffeine and sugar (they activate the fight or flight response).
- Practise deep breathing or diaphragmatic breathing with her.
- Send her a link to The BRAVE Program (see Resources).

DEPRESSION

Research suggests that one in five young people aged 16–24 suffers from depression that is distressing enough to justify seeking professional help. The symptoms can range from an ongoing low mood and lack of energy, to severe disruptions to sleep and appetite, extreme mood swings and suicidal thinking.

Any such condition impacts on a young woman's ability to get through her day. Worse, it can erode the foundation of her relationships with family, friends and teachers. While clinical experience suggests that early diagnosis and prompt treatment are effective, many young people who experience a mental disorder never seek professional help. This is because many young people do not know where to go for help, and parents and teachers don't know what signs to look for.

Depression warning signs

- Frequent, unexplained sadness or tearfulness
- Persistent low energy
- A preoccupation with morbid or lawless themes
- A lack of connection with family and friends
- Extreme sensitivity to rejection or failure
- Increased irritability, anger or hostility
- Frequent complaints of physical illnesses, such as stomach-aches or menstrual problems
- A major change in eating or sleeping habits
- Self-destructive or self-harming behaviours

What to do

- Don't dismiss her behaviour as 'normal' adolescent mood swings.
- Try to engage your daughter in conversation about how she is feeling about herself and her life, and listen carefully to what she says without judgement – this is very important (see page 108 for listening tips).
- If she is complaining of physical illness, don't accuse her of faking. Seek help from a GP and obtain a full physical examination with blood tests.
- If the GP suggests referral to a psychologist or psychiatrist, ensure she attends the sessions. (And remember that they are private. She does not have

to tell you what is discussed in the sessions.)
- Encourage regular exercise, good sleep habits and a healthy diet.
- Encourage her to take part in activities that once gave her pleasure (walks, movies) and be gently insistent if your invitation is refused.
- NEVER ignore any remarks about suicide: report them to a GP or psychologist as soon as possible. If you feel the situation is urgent, call 000 immediately.

In many cases, seeing a mental health professional (psychologist, counsellor or psychiatrist) is sufficient to help a young person recover from depression. In more severe cases, it may be necessary to consider medication, though if your daughter is under 18, this decision must always be made under the guidance of a psychiatrist or paediatrician – not simply your GP – as there is still some debate over the use of antidepressants in paediatric populations. Antidepressants may have only minimal to modest efficacy in the treatment of depression in young people, and have also been associated with psychiatric and emotional side effects, many of which appear to be more common among young people, including increased risk of suicidality, aggression and emotional blunting. Fluoxetine (Prozac) has a slightly better risk–benefit profile than the others, and, at the time of writing, is the only antidepressant approved for the treatment of depressive disorders in children and adolescents in the UK, USA and Australia.

EATING DISORDERS

This generation is more media savvy than any preceding one and has been raised on images of sassy 'girl heroes'. At the same time, today's ideal stick-thin look can contribute to body image problems and eating disorders.

There are several factors that affect eating behaviours during adolescence, including changing body shape and increased self-awareness, new sexual feelings, and risk-taking tendencies. In addition, there is the ubiquitous media imagery that encourages unrealistic body images. While the proportion of the population that is overweight is increasing, young people are surrounded on all sides by images of 'ideal' but impossibly thin body shapes.

There are two types of eating disorders that are most likely to begin in adolescence: anorexia and bulimia. Anorexia nervosa, which affects 0.5–1 per cent of young women, is a serious and potentially life-threatening illness involving the restriction of food intake and weight. Bulimia nervosa, which affects 1–5 per cent of young women, is characterised by repeated episodes of binge eating followed by compensatory behaviours, such as vomiting or excessive exercise.

Eating disorder warning signs
- A marked increase or decrease in weight with no medical cause
- The rise of abnormal eating habits, such as severe dieting or secretive bingeing
- An extreme preoccupation with weight and body image

- Compulsive or excessive exercising
- Self-induced vomiting, or excessive use of laxatives, diet pills or diuretics

A young woman with anorexia is often in denial and will most likely reject offers of help, preferring to isolate herself. She may be on the constant lookout for opportunities to secretly exercise and to hide food rather than consume it, which can make it very difficult for parents to monitor her eating habits.

What to do

- Remain composed and always talk calmly.
- Seek professional help. Start with your GP, who can refer you to a disordered-eating clinic at the nearest hospital.
- Don't blame yourself or your parenting.
- Don't blame her for what is going on. And never give up on her, no matter how difficult things get.
- Don't comment on her appearance. Even if you think you are being positive, whatever you say is likely to be misinterpreted.
- Don't try to force her to eat, or make mealtimes a major drama. If you are working with a health professional, you will have a strategy for how supportive and assertive you need to be at meal times – and importantly, what she knows she can expect from you.

SELF-HARM

The term 'self-harm' is most often associated with cutting but it can also involve overdosing on over-the-counter and prescription drugs, swallowing harmful chemicals such as bleach, or banging or hitting the body. Most parents I encounter whose daughters are self-harming are terrified that their daughters want to end their lives, but in most cases, the young women are trying to distract themselves from overwhelming emotional pain. In my experience, many young women who self-harm are using it to try to cope with destructive relationships at home or school, or some kind of emotional trauma such as a breakup, the death of a relative or other pressures.

Self-harm is not just 'attention seeking', although some girls do use it as a way of letting others know that they aren't coping. Other reasons young women have given for their self-harm include:

- trying to express complicated or hidden feelings
- communicating a need for some support
- proving to themselves that they are not invisible
- feeling in control
- getting an immediate sense of relief from the pain.

Unsurprisingly, parents confronted with a daughter who is self-harming generally panic and become frightened, confused or even angry. It is crucial that you do not share these reactions with your daughter. She is already feeling isolated, helpless and desperate and needs you to be strong enough to assist her in getting help.

It is important not to ignore her self-harming, as there is a good chance she may be experiencing anxiety or has depression, so if she stops self-harming, she may replace this behaviour with an eating disorder or substance abuse (such as drinking or taking drugs). Self-harm is never the whole picture. On a brighter note, I have seen many clients simply grow out of self-harming as they develop the skills to manage their wellbeing.

What to do

- Try to stay calm, be a role model and show that you can manage *your* difficult emotions.
- Act on your instincts. If you suspect that your daughter is self-harming, ask her, 'Have you ever felt so bad that you have hurt yourself on purpose?' Upon the discovery, ask, 'What happened?' Reassure her that you understand, that you are going to get her professional help and that it's going to be okay.
- Offer a hug (for at least 20 seconds). If your hug request is denied, you can hug with your words.
- Take her to see your GP and/or contact an adolescent mental health service such as headspace to find a practitioner experienced in adolescent mental health.

SUICIDE AND SUICIDAL BEHAVIOURS

In the early months of 2016, while putting the finishing touches to this book, the Australian Bureau of Statistics released the latest suicide statistics. While the suicide rate for young men is now showing signs of decline, the suicide rate for young women, although much lower, has doubled since 2008. Over the past decade, an increasing number of studies and reports document an evident and abrupt fall in teenage girls' mental health. From a clinical point of view, I cannot remember seeing so many stressed and depressed girls so early in adolescence. We cannot ignore the fact that, for an increasing number of Australian girls, the journey through adolescence is manifestly miserable.

Girls with mental health problems do less well in school and are more likely to abuse alcohol and other drugs, engage in bullying behaviours, and attempt and complete suicide. It is not news to anyone in the mental health sector that anxiety and depression are two of the leading causes that underpin the deteriorating mental health of young people in this country. This is a much-needed alarm for parents and doctors to look into the signs of depression and anxiety among young women so that appropriate services can be provided on time. This is everyone's problem.

Suicide and suicidal thinking are associated with a variety of biological, social and psychological factors, including traumatic life events and/or mental health conditions, such as depression, anxiety disorders and borderline personality disorder. Resilience, self-esteem, connectedness, belonging, supportive environments and positive life events can be valuable safeguards against the effects of trauma and mental health conditions. Parents need to realise that most suicidal girls don't want to die. Rather, they are usually experiencing extreme distress and/or unbearable emotional pain and are looking for a way out. With support they can find better ways to manage their distress and get through the crisis.

While it is clear that young people in Australia are more knowledgeable about mental health issues than they were a generation ago, it seems that knowledge is not enough. An opportunity exists to build on this knowledge with concise instructions about seeking help, managing stress and offering crisis support. This must include strategies that embrace the use of new and emerging technologies. Instead of demonising smartphone apps, wearable devices and social media, we need to use this technology to reach those most at risk, including people who are unemployed, homeless, Indigenous, gay, lesbian, bisexual, transgender, intersex or questioning and those who are geographically isolated or have a disability.

The key message for all parents reading this book is that the vast majority of young women who take their own lives have a history of mental illness – some diagnosed, some not. The most common mental illness associated with suicide is depression. So suicide prevention is really all about depression awareness. Early diagnosis and prompt treatment of suicidal behaviours and depression combined with good follow-up is essential.

A Quick Quiz

I've included this quiz to check if you've been paying attention. Only joking. I'm actually hoping you'll use this quiz as a jumping-off point for a discussion with your daughter about some of the development issues raised in this book. Perhaps she can give you the quiz *before* you read the book.

1. How many brain cells are there in the brain of an average 12-year-old girl?
   a) 100 billion
   b) 200 billion
   c) 300 billion
   d) 500 billion

   Answer: A

A massive growth spurt in childhood means that a girl's brain is already 90–95 per cent of adult size by age six. By the age of 12, she has 100 billion brain cells, but her brain still needs some intensive remodelling before it can function as an adult brain. This renovation happens during the teenage years and right up until the early to mid-20s, and is responsible for the impulsive and peer-driven behaviour characteristic of the teenage years. To respond in a developmentally appropriate way, parents need to listen and negotiate, but also set reasonable and fair limits and boundaries, engage in active monitoring and supervision, and use consequential learning (see chapter 9).

2. What is the minimum amount of sleep a 13-year-old girl requires?
    a) 7 hours
    b) 8 hours
    c) 9 hours
    d) 10 hours

Answer: C

Research on sleep patterns suggests that teenage girls need nine hours of sleep every night – yet in reality they are getting as little as five hours a night. Chronic sleep deprivation can have dramatic effects on a teenager's health and wellbeing, including her moods, her weight and her academic performance. Sleep is a non-negotiable behaviour, and parents need to be firm on this. Make the bedroom a haven for sleep – cool, dark and quiet, with a ban on technology in the bedroom at night-time. Back-lit screens inhibit the flow of melatonin (the sleep hormone), so charging devices away from the bedroom is ideal. Princess B won't like removing the digital lifeline to her peers, the most important people in her life for the next few years, but parents need to stay firm on this.

3. **What is the most important energy source for a 14-year-old girl's brain?**
   a) Oxygen
   b) Glucose
   c) Electricity
   d) Steak

Answer: B

Glucose is the preferred fuel for your brain, nervous system, kidneys and red blood cells, and the fuel you use first when you start to exercise. It is made when our bodies break down carbohydrates. Carbs can be simple (sugar, honey, lollies, soft drinks, fruit juice, etc.) or complex. Simple carbs enter your bloodstream quickly and are either used up immediately or stored as fat. Typically, they offer little or no nutritional value and, in fact, contribute to poor health. Complex, starch-based carbohydrates include cereals, flour, rice and veggies such as sweet corn and pumpkin. The energy from whole-grain cereals and vegetables typically takes longer to enter the bloodstream and provides a more sustained form of energy. That's why a breakfast of whole-grain cereal or toast keeps us firing on all cylinders until lunchtime.

A UK study reported that 39 per cent of girls skipped breakfast some or all of the time, with many of them wrongly believing that it would help them lose weight. Children who miss breakfast are more likely to snack on sugary foods later in the day, and are at risk of diabetes later in life. Many also experience difficulty concentrating in lessons, and become lethargic and exhibit behavioural problems. Like sleep, this is a non-negotiable issue (see page 131 for more information).

4   In 1860, the average age at menarche (a girl's first period) in the UK was 15 years old. What is it today?

    a) 14–15 years
    b) 13–14 years
    c) 12–13 years
    d) 11–12 years

    Answer: C

Today's girls are going through puberty much earlier than previous generations. The first signs of puberty, such as breast buds and pubic hair, occur up to three years before menarche – meaning that girls are starting puberty these days at around age nine. This means girls can look physically older than they are. See chapter 2 for more about the effects of early puberty.

5.   According to a 2015 study by the American Psychological Association, how many times a day on average did teenagers send or receive a text message?

    a) 67
    b) 167
    c) 267
    d) 367

Answer: B

The study also found that while girls don't text more frequently than boys, they are more likely to be negatively affected academically by compulsive texting behaviours. This is because boys tend to use digital technology to convey information, while girls use it for social interaction and to nurture relationships. Teenage girls are also more likely than boys to ruminate with others, or engage in obsessive, preoccupied thinking, which is more distracting. Parents need to talk to their children early on about treating people with respect when texting and never writing anything that they would not want the four Ps to see – parents, police, the school principal or a paedophile.

6. In the last five annual surveys conducted by Mission Australia, what single issue consistently rated number one as girls' biggest worry?
   a) Body image
   b) Bullying
   c) School and study problems
   d) Coping with stress

Answer: D

Having the capacity to face, overcome and be transformed by adversity is a major predictor of wellbeing in the future. It also predicts the child's ability to maintain, obtain and retain friendships, which is also an indicator of good psychological health. Parents need to ask themselves if their daughters exhibit competence in anger management, conflict resolution and decision-making.

The use of online resources such as Mood Gym, a free, cognitive behavioural therapy (CBT) based intervention designed to build resilience and coping skills, is highly recommended in early adolescence. The five MoodGYM modules, completed at her own pace, teach your daughter the connection between thoughts and feelings and how to change moods. This is great 'psychological insurance' for her.

7. In the 2013 National Survey of Australian Secondary Students and Sexual Health, what percentage of young people expressed significant dissatisfaction with sex education at schools?

   a) 25 per cent
   b) 35 per cent
   c) 50 per cent
   d) 65 per cent

   Answer: C

Sex education is the process of acquiring information and forming attitudes and beliefs about sex, sexual identity, relationships and intimacy. Sex education is also about developing young people's skills so that they can make informed choices about their behaviour and feel confident and competent about acting on these choices. According to the La Trobe University survey cited above, female students most commonly sourced information on sexual health from female friends (51 per cent), followed by internet websites (47 per cent), the school sexual health program (45 per cent), mothers (43 per cent) and

184 - The Princess Bitchface Syndrome 2.0

doctors (32 per cent). Moreover, 50 per cent said that sex education at school was irrelevant to their real experiences, lacked relationship advice and lacked discussion of same-sex issues.

Sexual health is a public health issue, and since we know that school-based sex education is not meeting young people's needs all of the time, and young people need the skills to identify good-quality, accurate information, parents must step up to the plate. For ideas about how to do this, see chapter 11.

8. Which of the following conditions in adolescent females has the highest mortality rate?
    a) Anorexia nervosa
    b) Depression
    c) Schizophrenia
    d) Anxiety

Answer: A

Anorexia nervosa is a psychological illness with devastating physical consequences. The illness is characterised by low body weight and body image distortion with an obsessive fear of gaining weight, which manifests itself through depriving the body of food. Based on international data, the lifetime prevalence for females is between 0.3 per cent and 1.5 per cent, and between 0.1 per cent and 0.5 per cent for males. The onset of anorexia usually occurs in adolescence, with a median age of onset of 17 years, and it often coincides with increased levels of exercise. It has the highest mortality rate of all psychiatric illnesses; extreme food restriction can lead to starvation, malnutrition and a dangerously low body weight. All of these factors can lead to a host of health problems and, in some cases, death.

9. **According to research undertaken by Bond University in 2015, what proportion of Australian video/computer gamers were female?**

    a) 17 per cent
    b) 27 per cent
    c) 37 per cent
    d) 47 per cent

    Answer: D

The typical Australian gamer looks very different to the stereotype of a teenage boy. The report found the average age of gamers had increased to 33 years, up from 24 in 2005, and women were close to equal representation in the gaming community, making up 47 per cent of gamers. Research shows that women rapidly adopted games between 2005 and 2009, when gaming apps arrived on smartphones, and it is predicted more will join as game genres diversify. Parents should monitor the content of their daughter's video games, and follow age recommendations. The younger their daughter is, the more parents should keep them away from violent and explicit content.

10. A 2004 study published in the Medical Journal of Australia showed that the rate of deliberate self-harm in young women was 11 per cent. What was the greatest predictor of this behaviour?

   a) Being bullied
   b) Having a friend or family member who had self-harmed
   c) Being from a different cultural background
   d) Being diagnosed with a depressive illness

Answer: B

This Australian study showed that the factor most significantly associated with increased deliberate self-harm in the previous year in females was exposure to self-harm in friends or family members. Other factors included sexual orientation worries, low self-esteem and distressing life events. Self-harm comes in many forms and can be very damaging to a person's physical and mental health. It is most often used as a way of coping with difficult emotions, rather than an indication of suicidality. In my experience, many young women who self-harm are trying to cope with adverse experiences or destructive relationships. Self-harm is not just 'attention seeking', although some girls do use it as a way of letting others know they aren't coping. Other reasons young women have given for their self-harm include trying to express complicated or hidden feelings, communicating a need for some support, proving to themselves that they are not invisible, feeling in control, and getting an immediate sense of relief. Parents confronted with their daughter's self-harm generally become very frightened, confused, angry and panicked. Chapter 15 outlines ways to identify and deal with self-harm.

11. A 2006 New Zealand study found that one-third of students with which particular medical condition have had suicidal thoughts?

a) Diabetes
b) Asthma
c) Arthritis
d) Acne

Answer: D

Acne can have a profound social and psychological impact on young people, an outcome that needs far greater attention than it currently receives. Even mild acne can be significantly disabling. New research has revealed the impact the common skin condition has on self-esteem and confidence. A 2015 survey, commissioned by the British Skin Foundation, found that one-fifth of people with acne have contemplated suicide, and more than half (56 per cent) have been the victim of verbal abuse. Severe depression from acne has also resulted in attempted and completed suicide. Parents, friends and school personnel ought to be alert to worrying statements such as, 'I don't want to wake up in the morning', 'I'd be better off dead', 'I'm worthless' or 'You'd be better off without me'. Severe depression and suicidality may also be associated with acne treatment (particularly isotretinoin). If prescribed, regular monitoring of mental health is suggested.

12. **According to a study by Young and Well CRC in 2014, which of the following is true about same-sex-attracted young people compared to their heterosexual peers?**

    a) They are 6 times more likely to try to take their own lives.
    b) They are 5 times more likely to use illicit drugs.
    c) They are 3 times more likely to be bullied at school.
    d) They are 4 times more likely to suffer a major depressive illness.

    Answer: A

LGBTIQ young people are six times more likely to try to take their own lives compared to other young people, largely because of a lack of acceptance and bullying by members of their family, school or the wider community. In the online national survey mentioned above, 41 per cent of respondents had thoughts about self-harm and/or suicide, 33 per cent had harmed themselves, and 16 per cent had attempted suicide. Support for both the young person and their family is vital to avoid the potential mental health impacts as outlined. See chapter 11 for more information.

13. **What is the greatest predictor of a future suicide attempt or completed suicide?**

    a) A history of self-harm
    b) A history of depression
    c) A history of previous attempts
    d) A history of anxiety disorders

Answer: C

A previous suicide attempt is the strongest predictor of a future suicide attempt or completed suicide. There is evidence to suggest that up to 25 per cent of those treated in emergency departments for a suicide attempt will make a future attempt, with 5–10 per cent eventually completing suicide. Repeated attempts are more likely if previous attempts have been medically serious. For more about mental health and suicide, see chapter 15.

14. The National Health and Medical Research Council (NHMRC) issued guidelines in 2009 suggesting that young people should not drink until what age?

    a) 14
    b) 16
    c) 18
    d) 21

Answer: C

Evidence is emerging about the dangers of drinking in the teenage years, so the advice is that young people should not drink alcohol *at all* until at least the age of 18. Drinking alcohol contributes to the three leading causes of death in adolescence – unintentional injury (mainly car accidents), suicide and homicide – and is associated with risky sexual behaviour, academic failure and adverse behaviour patterns. Parents play a very important role in preventing and responding to underage drinking. Communication, clear expectations and boundaries, consistent discipline and minimal family conflict all contribute to children initiating alcohol use at later ages. Parents should also consider the ways in which they might avoid conveying positive attitudes to drinking, and model responsible drinking behaviours.

15. According to the National Drug and Alcohol Research Centre, what is the most commonly used drug in drink spiking?

   a) Gamma hydroxybutyrate (GHB)
   b) Cocaine
   c) Rohypnol
   d) Ethanol (ethyl alcohol)

Answer: D

The public perception is that drugs such as Rohypnol or GHB are commonly used to spike drinks. In fact, this is not supported by toxicology results, which indicate that alcohol itself is the main culprit. Rohypnol, a brand name for the benzodiazepine flunitrazepam, was in fact withdrawn from sale in Australia in 1998. Alcohol is relatively cheap, easy to obtain and legal to use, and can be added to drinks without necessarily arousing suspicion. Where drugs are used, sediment may remain in the glass or strong smells or tastes will often be apparent. In contrast, relatively tasteless alcohols such as vodka and tequila may be less easily detected. Drink spiking, even when it is done as a joke, is illegal. Parents can talk to their daughters about how to avoid drink spiking – see chapter 13 for information.

16. Which of the following drugs cause the most deaths in young people in Australia?

    a) Heroin
    b) Alcohol
    c) Ice
    d) Ecstasy

    Answer: B

While the media focus is often on illicit drugs like ice and heroin, the fact is that more young Australians die from alcohol than from any other drug. Recently introduced legislation in Victoria means that it is against the law to serve alcohol in a private home to anyone under 18, unless they have a parent or guardian's permission. This law is part of an effort to reduce the harm of drinking for young people and their families and friends. See chapter 13 for more on alcohol and teens.

17. What is the most appropriate response when your daughter comes home unexpectedly, and without permission, with a tongue stud?

    a) Invite her to take it out or find somewhere else to live.
    b) Tell her how nice it looks and suggest getting another one.
    c) Get a pair of pliers and ask her to open her mouth.
    d) Tell her she must be really pleased with it, but you'd like to discuss your concerns, including the health risks.

Answer: D

This is one of those situations where you need to choose your battles. Mouth piercings do carry health risks but these can be properly managed. Getting a GP to discuss the health risks with your daughter is a sensible option – these include infection (which can be serious, such as hepatitis C), thick scars or allergic reactions. There are jurisdictional differences in laws regarding both intimate (e.g. genitalia, anal region, nipples) and non-intimate (e.g. nose, tongue, face) piercings. In many states, it is illegal to perform an intimate piercing, even with parental consent, on a person under the age of 18 years. Some piercers have their own age restrictions and may ask for parental consent for young people under a certain age, even if the law in your area does not require this. If her school has a 'no tongue stud' rule then your daughter must obey that rule.

18. Which of the following is the most appropriate response when your teenage daughter (during an argument) says she wishes her sister were dead?
    a) 'You sound angry, tell me about it.'
    b) 'Don't say that – your sister has some wonderful gifts.'
    c) 'I don't like her either, let's leave!'
    d) 'Just ignore her.'

Answer: A

Until their brains are fully developed in their mid-20s, teenagers may often react emotionally to situations and blurt out things they don't mean. Anger is a normal emotion to experience, and it is not helpful to believe it can just be avoided at all costs. It is especially normal for siblings to fight and be angry at one another. Parents can avoid overreacting and look for the meaning behind the emotion, and discuss this with their teen. There are also plenty of ways to help minimise sibling rivalry (see page 123).

19. **What is the best response if your daughter comes home sporting black from head to toe, except for green tips in her gothic black hair?**

   a) Be totally honest – laugh.
   b) Order her to grow up and take off that ridiculous outfit.
   c) Stay calm and ask her how her day has been.
   d) Ask what time the carnival begins.

   Answer: C

Identity development is an important part of adolescence. Teenage girls will try on one 'mask' after another in order to find one that fits. Her reasons for dressing this way may be due to peer pressure, a desire for rebellion or both. Your job as a parent is to observe and encourage, not to criticise and judge. This is not a battle worth fighting – with the exception of when you object to the clothing on the basis of how revealing it is. To find a solution, it's important to find a good time to talk to her like an adult and be open and honest about your feelings, all in a non-judgemental way. Talk about how you can find a solution that would work for both of you, and be prepared to either compromise or clearly identify what you will not compromise about. Insist that she resists changing again after leaving the house as this is childish and fosters a lack of trust between the two of you. If there is clothing that has been identified as completely unacceptable, it should not be in her possession.

20. Your Year 9 daughter is going out with her Year 10 boyfriend. You want her home at a reasonable hour. What two things should you do?

   a) Drive her there and back.
   b) Set a non-negotiable time and text her every 30 seconds if she is late.
   c) Discuss and agree on a safe and fair time to be home.
   d) Agree on a reasonable consequence if she's late.
   e) Ask her boyfriend to sign a contract and leave a deposit.

   Answer: C & D

Reasonable boundaries should be discussed beforehand, and consequences, too. If she does seriously stuff up and breaches your trust, try not to let your first reaction be one of anger and betrayal. Even though it often feels personal, it's not a reflection on you or your parenting. Instead, enforce the agreed consequence and, in doing so, help her learn how to take responsibility.

Resources

PARENTING

Raising Children Network
http://raisingchildren.net.au

Beyond Blue Healthy Families
https://healthyfamilies.beyondblue.org.au/age-13

Help lines
Australian Capital Territory (02) 6287 3833
New South Wales 1300 130 052
Queensland/Northern Territory 1300 301 300
South Australia 1300 364 100
Tasmania 1300 808 178
Victoria 132 289
Western Australia 1800 654 432

RELATIONSHIPS

Stepfamilies Australia
www.stepfamily.org.au
(03) 9663 6733

1800MYLINE

1800 695 463

Offers 24/7 support and advice to young people about relationships or relationship violence.

Men's Line Australia

www.mensline.org.au
1300 78 99 78

Offers telephone and online support, information and referral for men dealing with relationship problems as well as a free call-back service (9 a.m. to 11 p.m.) and free 30-minute online text and video counselling sessions.

Family Relationships Advice Line

www.familyrelationships.gov.au
1800 050 321

Offers advice, information and referrals for all families, whether together or separated (8 a.m. to 8 p.m. weekdays, 10 a.m. to 4 p.m. Saturdays, except national public holidays).

BULLYING AND ONLINE SAFETY

Bullying. No Way!

https://bullyingnoway.gov.au
Offers information and advice for kids, parents and educators on bullying and what to do.

Website for the Office of the Children's eSafety

https://esafety.gov.au

Commissioner provides online safety education and a complaints service for cyber bullying and illegal content.

ANXIETY AND DEPRESSION

Online self-help programs

The BRAVE Program
https://brave4you.psy.uq.edu.au
An interactive, online program developed by beyondblue and the University of Queensland to help prevent and treat childhood and adolescent anxiety. The programs are free, and provide ways for children and teenagers to better cope with their worries. There are also programs for parents.

MoodGYM
https://moodgym.anu.edu.au
A free, interactive self-help program run by the Australian National University that provides cognitive behaviour therapy (CBT) training in order to help users prevent and cope with depression.

Reachout
http://au.reachout.com/all-about-feeling-anxious
Reachout.com is a youth mental health site that offers excellent information about anxiety.

e-couch
https://ecouch.anu.edu.au
Also run by the Australian National University, this program

offers free online treatment for anxiety disorders and depression that you do at your own pace. It helps you to identify and change the patterns of thinking and behaviour that either trigger your anxiety or prevent you from overcoming it.

Helplines

Kids Helpline

www.kidshelp.com.au/teens
1800 551 800
Offers 24/7 telephone support for young people up to 25; web chat times vary from state to state.

Youth Beyondblue

www.youthbeyondblue.com
1300 224 636
Offers 24/7 telephone support for young people up to 25; web chat 3 p.m. to 12 a.m.

eheadspace

www.eheadspace.org.au
1800 650 890
Has qualified youth counsellors available for telephone and online counselling 9 a.m. to 1 a.m. 7 days.

The Samaritans

www.thesamaritans.org.au
13 52 47
Offers 24/7 telephone counselling and support.

Sane Australia Helpline

www.sane.org
1800 187 263
Free information and referrals for mental health; 9 a.m. to
5 p.m. weekdays (including public holidays).

SUICIDE

Lifeline

www.lifeline.org.au/Get-Help
13 11 14
Offers 24/7 telephone crisis support; web chat 8 p.m. to
4 a.m.

Suicide Call Back Service

1300 659 467
Provides 24/7 crisis counselling (phone and web chat) to
people at risk of suicide, carers of someone who is suicidal,
and those bereaved by suicide across Australia.

Support After Suicide

www.supportaftersuicide.org.au/find-related-organisations
This Jesuit website has links to the dozens of bereavement
support services across Australia.

(Salvos) Hope for Life

http://suicideprevention.salvos.org.au
1300 467 354
Offers 24/7 bereavement support (run by the Salvation
Army).

Suicide Line (Victoria)

www.suicideline.org.au

1300 651 251

Offers support for people who are feeling suicidal or concerned about another person who may be suicidal. Also for people who are grieving or emotionally affected after a suicide,

ALCOHOL AND OTHER DRUGS

Family Drug Support

www.fds.org.au

1300 368 186

Offers 24/7 information and referral.

Counselling Online

www.counsellingonline.org.au

1800 888 236

Offers 24/7 drug and alcohol counselling and advice (telephone and web chat).

Alcoholics Anonymous Australia

www.aa.org.au

1300 222 222

Offers 24/7 alcohol counselling via telephone; also runs Australia-wide group meetings to assist alcoholics in their recovery.

Cannabis Information and Helpline

https://ncpic.org.au

1800 30 40 50
Offers advice and support 11 a.m. to 7 p.m. weekdays including public holidays.

YSAS (Victoria)

1800 458 685
Youth Support and Advocacy Service provides youth drug and alcohol support and advice weekdays from 9 a.m. to 8 p.m.

GENDER AND SEXUALITY

Minus 18

https://minus18.org.au
Australia's largest youth-led organisation for gay, lesbian, bisexual and trans youth.

It Gets Better

www.itgetsbetter.org
Video sharing site set up by Dan Savage for LGBTIQ people to share experiences.

PFLAG

www.pflagaustralia.org.au
Support organisation for parents, families and friends of lesbian and gay people.

Out & Online

www.outandonline.org.au
Provides online self-help modules for same-sex-attracted young people who are experiencing anxiety or depression.

Index

In his work as a family psychologist, Michael Carr-Gregg has noticed
a worrying trend in our modern parenting styles, which sees kids running
riot and parents running for cover.

In *Strictly Parenting*, Michael asks parents to take a good hard look at the
way they are parenting – to toughen up and stop trying to be their kids'
best friends. He offers practical evidence-based solutions on how to take
back the reins and start making the most of the precious family years.

Young people today enter puberty earlier than ever before and leave home later. The good news is that teenagers aren't impossible to live with, especially if parents adopt the common-sense strategies set out in this book.

Surviving Adolescents is a clear and down-to-earth manual full of advice on all the thorny issues that confront families with teenagers, including sexuality, risky behaviours, laziness, school and study problems, and many more. It is the sensible, sanity-saving guide every household needs.